WORKING CLASS

MAKING THE TRADES COOL AGAIN

NICK KASIK

iUniverse®

WORKING CLASS
MAKING THE TRADES COOL AGAIN

iUniverse books may be ordered through booksellers or by contacting:

iUniverse
1663 Liberty Drive
Bloomington, IN 47403
www.iuniverse.com
844-349-9409

Because of the dynamic nature of the Internet, any web addresses or links contained in this book may have changed since publication and may no longer be valid. The views expressed in this work are solely those of the author and do not necessarily reflect the views of the publisher, and the publisher hereby disclaims any responsibility for them.

Any people depicted in stock imagery provided by Getty Images are models, and such images are being used for illustrative purposes only. Certain stock imagery © Getty Images.

ISBN: 978-1-6632-4123-8 (sc)
ISBN: 978-1-6632-4133-7 (hc)
ISBN: 978-1-6632-4124-5 (e)

Print information available on the last page.

iUniverse rev. date: 06/23/2022

CONTENTS

INTRODUCTION

The TV show Working Class was developed to bring attention to the trades, and to promote vocational careers. We celebrate the technological advancements and skills that are required to work in the trades, illustrating just how out of touch with the trade's society has become.

Over the course of the show, we have highlighted many different trades, as well as the stories of the interesting people who work in these trades each day. We illustrate how technologically advanced the trades people are and invite you on a journey to understand how we got to where we are.

In this book we step back in time to the beginning and examine when this young country was born out of hard work, grit, and determination. We survived a revolution, a civil war, a great depression, the dust bowl, prohibition, two world wars and a host of other hardships. Through all of this, the strength of this great country was built on the backs of the working class, who got up early, got their hands dirty, and did the work of this great nation. These are the people who shower at the end of the day, after their work is done, rather than in the morning before they go to work. But somewhere along the way, we seem to have lost sight of this, and the pendulum has swung away from our proud roots.

If you look at the general work force today, and certainly the younger work force, you will find at least two generations of people who simply were not taught what it takes to build a nation, an economy, and a solid cultural foundation. It's not their fault. No one told them. They were taught not to get dirty or work hard. Society taught them they could do as little as possible and make a lot of money as quickly as possible. And then, if something doesn't go that way, it is the fault of society.

So now we have a workforce that is broken and confused. We have a generation of managers with no one to manage, and a younger generation of people who were lied to. They were sold the promise of prosperity and success, in exchange for a college degree. Instead, they were left with degrees in fields that have no jobs, and mountains of debt, while the colleges and universities continued to grow and prosper.

I the meantime, everyone forgot about the trades, the craftsmen, the vocational arts… Yes arts. The art of being a craftsman is quickly becoming forgotten. The trades are not second class. They are not a fallback plan in case you cannot get into college. The trades are the arts of working with your hands to create beautiful and functional creations that improve the quality of life in a direct and significant way.

Our society, led by our educational institutions for decades dating back to the 1980s and earlier, have worked to line the pockets of the elite, convincing kids that college is the only path to success. And yes, while it is a path to success, it is not the only path, and we ought not stand for this any longer.

We will look back at the great resignation, as a time in our history, where this lost generation stood up and said, "No More"! It will be a time in our history where we corrected the trajectory of progress, and the masses will begin turning back to entrepreneurship, trades, and crafts, placing more value on pride, experiences, and traditions than on money, status, and perceived success.

The TV show Working Class takes us on this journey each episode, and here in this book we dive deeper into the history, present and the future… Deeper than we can do in a 30-minute episode.

CHAPTER ONE

The Way It Was

Isn't it amazing, as we get a little older, how certain things from our youth we thought to be a useless waste of time, now become somewhat more interesting, and even validate our experiences in everyday life? Of course, we all remember our high school history class (yeah, right). Well, even if we don't remember the class, we do remember having to go to history class, and as much as we hated history as a kid, we actually do remember the history of how this great country got its start. We recall the stories of the fearless patriots Paul Revere, John Adams, Ben Franklin, and many of the other founding fathers of this country. And while we didn't really care as kids, we did still manage to retain a broad view of the history of this country.

But how many of us are aware of the Paul Revere that they failed to teach us about? Paul Revere, the craftsman and silversmith. Not only was Paul Revere an accomplished silversmith, but so was his father, Paul Revere Sr., who he had apprenticed under for many years. Of course, we all know that Ben Franklin was a master of many crafts. But did you know that John Adams was an accomplished shoemaker, or John Adams the farmer? These great men were not only the architects of this great country, but they were also part of a colonial craftsman tradition that was more than a two hundred years in the making.

When colonists first came to America, they had to be extremely self-sufficient. Anything that they couldn't make for themselves had to be imported from Europe, and the cost of transportation made such imports just too expensive. Shoes, nails, pots, bottles, guns, tools, clothing, and most of the day to day necessities of life, were at first brought over on ships. But even as the early ships brought goods for the colonists, craftsmen were setting up shop, and establishing their crafts locally.

At this time, long before the Industrial Revolution, everything was made by the hand of craftsmen who often specialized in a single craft such as barrel making, glassblowing or carpentry. However, the conditions of the first colonies required a lot more flexibility on the part of craftsmen who were often forced by circumstance, to expand beyond their initial area's expertise. Towns were small and scattered, which limited the market for specialized products. Thus, a barrel-maker might be forced into making furniture, fencing, and other wood products, in addition to barrels.

Prior to the 19th Century, people spent their whole lives working, and as food was most important, the great majority of the people were farmers. If they had schooling, it consisted of a few weeks each winter (when there was less field work to be done) and lasted usually no more than eight years. The young were taught the basics of how to write, reading, and enough math to calculate wages and make change.

As they grew up, the children of working families were expected to help with chores suited to their strength, running errands, carrying water, bringing in firewood, tending younger brothers and sisters. Boys soon learned to milk cows, feed the pigs, clean stables, and chop wood. Girls helped their mothers cook, clean, sew, tend garden, bake bread, and the like. Depending on size and strength, boys sometime in their teens went to a job either because they wanted to, they thought it their duty, or they were pushed to it by their parents. If they were hard workers, frugal, and lucky, they in time might acquire some land for a small farm of their own, or tools and skill in using them for some sort of craft business.

Those less fortunate would work for others all of their working years. Few if any workers ever retired. That was a privilege of the wealthy and of successful professionals (lawyers, ministers, physicians). Workers whose health failed and could no longer work became dependent on their children or went on relief, moving to a publicly supported poor farm. These conditions were the same for all working families in most industries.

Boys who lived and worked on plantations usually began work in their mid-teens. They had no vocational school or other preparation for any job. They frequently started by working as a helper to their father, an uncle or older brother. These "helper" jobs were a sort of apprenticeship where they learned by watching and assisting. In this way boys discovered which jobs they liked or disliked, while the master craftsman noted those who looked promising for the more important and better paying jobs. The master craftsman also decided which boys were unlikely to be good at anything but supplying an extra hand. The prudent course for a young man was to learn something about several or even all of the various jobs on the plantation. Boys who were able to do anything that needed doing usually were assured steady work, and the quickest path to master craftsman status.

"Success" for most did not mean becoming wealthy, as that was so rare as to be unrealistic. To acquire a sustainable skill, a farm, or a job that was sufficient to support one's family in comfort, free of debt, was success for most working people. If their farm was large and fertile, it would carry the workman and his wife until their deaths. Usually, the child who agreed to stay and manage his parents' farm or business and live with and care for them in their declining years would inherit the property. The custom generally had been that the family home would pass the farm, or business to the oldest son.

This apprenticeship concept, which has been in place for centuries, continues today in this county, in similar form. And today, apprenticeship still continues to be an effective career path to mastering a craft and developing a successful career. When apprentices finish their training, they receive certificates of completion of apprenticeship. These are issued by the state apprenticeship agencies or, in those states not having such an agency, by the Bureau of Apprenticeship and Training in accordance with its recommended standards.

Joint apprenticeship committees, composed of representatives of management and labor, work together to develop and administer local apprenticeship training programs. In addition to local groups, national trade committees represent national organizations. With the help of the Bureau of Apprenticeship and Training, the national committees formulate policies on apprenticeship in the various trades and issue basic standards to be used by affiliated organizations.

The apprenticeship system has grown up with America. Like America, it is still growing and changing. Today it serves a far different nation from the one of colonial days. Many of these changes are attributed to scientific discoveries, new teaching methods, expanding industry, an increasing population, and a determination of people to live not only free, but equal. These are among the demands of our present-day technological and social systems to which apprenticeship is responding. To meet the need for changes, apprenticeships have been set up in new trades, and apprenticeships in many of the older trades have been updated. For example, in recent years a new apprenticeship program has been created to train electromechanical technicians. Workers in this expanding field create devices for mechanical control of all kinds of robotics, and specialized equipment.

Increasing numbers of women in apprenticeship reflect some of our changing attitudes about whose hands may do our skilled work. From 1900 to 1960, women held only 3 percent of the jobs in skilled trades, a figure that varied only during World War II. But by 1980 women had more than doubled their share, holding nearly 7 percent of the jobs in skilled trades.

Women in the trades account for nearly a million skilled trade workers. All skilled trades now report at least some women at work. They include such traditionally "men's" jobs as automobile mechanics, carpenters, heavy equipment mechanics, and telephone installation and repair workers. Despite this progress, many women still do not use the apprenticeship route to a well-paid occupation. The majority of women in apprenticeship are found in cosmetology and a few other trades. Through federally funded outreach programs, the Department of Labor, and local and national organizations are trying to broaden the horizons of women, counselors, prospective employers, and apprenticeship councils.

CHAPTER TWO

The Labor Union's Effect on the Craftsmen

The labor union movement in the United States originated much earlier than we may realize. During the 1790's some of the first unions were formed by carpenters, shoemakers, tailors, printers, and other trade groups in many large cities. Periodic work stoppages occurred during this time, although strike leaders were fined and imprisoned for what was termed "conspiracy to raise wages."

By the early 1800s, several trade unions had banded together to form the Mechanics' Union of Trade Associations, the first U.S. labor organization to unite workers in different crafts. Besides working to raise wages and improve working conditions, these united labor organizations supported certain social reforms, and perhaps the most important effect of these early unions was their introduction of political action. The decision of a Massachusetts court in 1842, stating that strikes to improve labor conditions were lawful and were not criminal conspiracies, was the spark that ensured labor unions a permanent place in our economy.

During the 1920's the trade union movement was on the decline, due largely to the depressions of the 20's and 30's. The election of Franklin D. Roosevelt to the Presidency in 1932 marked the beginning of stimulating new growth in the union movement. In 1933 the National Industrial Recovery Act was enacted, containing the law stipulated that "employees shall have the right to organize and to bargain collectively through representatives of their own choosing, and shall be free from the interference, restraint, or coercion of employers.

Since the 30s, America has had a love – hate relationship with the unions. Unions do provide much needed protection for workers, organized trade mentoring, education, organized apprenticeships, benefits, and stability in the workplace. Unions have been instrumental in improving the safety and working standards of all Americans in all industries with the implementation of standards. Union workers tend to be consistent and well trained.

Unions have provided mutual benefits in the construction industry, as contractors move from regional to national contractors. The unions offer contractors the ability to go anywhere in the country, knowing that they can have a competent and consistent workforce immediately on site.

However, on the other side of the coin, labor unions can easily become powerful and corrupt, sometimes forgetting their purpose and allegiance is to the workers, not the leaders of the union. Unions, by nature become politically driven because they become business driven entities which produce no product, only broker labor, and can hold an economy hostage. A perfect example of that is when the auto union damaged the American automotive industry by increasing cost and reducing production through their policies.

Because all Big 3 autoworkers are members of the union, the Big 3 had no choice but to continue paying the unions "for protection" from strikes and shutdowns. The high costs of paying the artificial wages and benefits "protection" demanded by the unions almost destroyed the City of Detroit and, to a larger extent, the economy and image of Michigan.

The foreign automakers continued to make advances in automobile quality by designing better vehicles, developing more efficient and effective manufacturing techniques. These companies began investing in US property and locating new plants in "union-free" Southern States. They were able to build vehicles as good, or better than Detroit, at a higher profit margin and lower cost due to the simple fact that they were not held hostage to the union's artificial backing.

The one undeniable advance that unions have given us, is the apprentice to journeyman to master training program. Unions have continued the several century old hierarchies of apprenticeship training, leading to journeyman production, culminating with master mentoring. This is a proven technique of training, oversight, and development that is underutilized, and highly successful. You are even beginning to see a hybrid version of this technique in traditional college education settings with the advancement of summer internships, which is nothing more than a temporary apprenticeship.

The bottom line on trade unions is that, like anything, too much of anything is a bad thing. Unions have their place in America when the members are in control of the leaders, and the focus of the union remains on the worker. When unions focus on the health and safety of the worker by instituting training programs, and working with business to negotiate reasonable wages that allow the companies to remain competitive, it works… When unions begin to focus on political issues, leadership becomes drunk with power, and the worker is no longer the focus, but a pawn, is when unions cease to provide a benefit to Americans.

CHAPTER THREE

Go To College, and Make Something of Yourself

G raduate high school, go to college, get a degree, get a good job, and make something of yourself! You don't want to end up like us, working all our lives, just getting by.

Remember hearing that from your parents? Most of us who are a product of the Baby Boomers and Gen-X heard that mandate as kids, and we did as we were told. We got those degrees, got a great job as a middle manager of something, sitting on our butts behind a desk, looking busy all day, pushing mountains of paper from one side of our desk to the other, barking at people all day on the phone, and pawing through hundreds of useless emails every day, never really accomplishing anything. Congratulations! We made it!

We were driven to succeed. Somehow, society convinced us that working with our hands, and that physical honest work, was somehow not honorable... Somehow, in the eyes of society, being a manager, lawyer, or doctor was in some way more decent than being a carpenter, plumber, farmer, or electrician.

Society convinced generations of kids to go into lifelong crushing debt, preparing for jobs that don't exist. Our educational system failed so many, by convincing everyone that white-collar professions are the only one's worth pursuing. The post-secondary educational system figured out how to get rich off forcing generations of kids into debt, and school funding was based on test scores, rather than skills. The value of that diploma was put above providing marketable skills.

So now, we have an entire workforce of managers, with no real marketable skills, no ability to think entrepreneurially, no trade skills, and no ability to go out and make on our own. The only skills we learned in college, and in our years working that middle management job, is how to be an employee... And some of us really didn't learn that very well.

I look back to my parents' generation, and the generations before. If they weren't satisfied with their lot in life, they changed it. If they hated their job, they worked like hell to get a better one. If they lost their jobs, they didn't sit on their butt collecting unemployment. They got another job. If there were no jobs, they created one, did odd jobs, or fell back on other skills to do what it took to put food on the table. They didn't sit in limbo, complaining that no one would hire them, and waiting for a job that might never come. They got off their butt and made it happen!

I will never forget what my dad told me with regard to college, and school. He said that he was glad that I was getting an education, and happy that I had the possibilities of new and better things in my life... But if things ever got bad, or there were no jobs, he knew that I learned the value of physical work, and that there is no job beneath you, because work is work. And he was right. I've delivered pizzas, cleaned sewers, done every type of construction, managed $200 million operations, and everything in between... And, honestly – doing the physical work was far more rewarding than any office job I ever had.

So why is it that we don't push our children to be truck drivers, plumbers, trash collectors, and concrete finishers? They are good honest jobs that pays as well as most entry level college graduate jobs. On average most community college trades have higher starting pay than four-year degree jobs. If the COVID pandemic taught us anything, it was which professions were essential, and which ones were not.

So why does our society seem to think that a bachelor's degree is better than an Associate degree? I can honestly tell you, that I gained ten times the knowledge with my AS degree and working in the trades compared to any college class I have ever taken. Associate degrees generally teach a marketable trade skill, and that's it. They don't waste your time with all the filler classes, while some may be interesting, they really have no marketable use in the real world… I'm sorry, but I've yet to find anyone with a liberal arts degree working in an essential liberal arts career. Their guidance counselor should have told them that they didn't need that liberal arts degree to get a fast-food job. They can get that right out of high school.

Here's the problem: the idea of graduating from a four-year college in the U.S. is so firmly ingrained in our culture that many of us have trouble envisioning anything else. It seems we send some kids off to college because there is nowhere else to put them. The campus is a convenient, although expensive, warehouse. How many kids are in college right now with an undeclared major? Think about that for a minute! It's nuts! We are paying tens of thousands of dollars a year sending our kids to school, not to become educated, but to figure out what they want to become educated in. And this is considered normal.

By clinging to the belief that education after high school can be found only at a four-year college campus, we exclude large portions of the American population from sharing in the nation's economic successes. In 1970, seven in every ten workers with a high school diploma or less were in the middle class. Why? Because people embraced becoming a craftsman or tradesman, learning the craft on the job, in the real world, from a successful craftsman, rather than in a classroom being taught by a professor who most likely never held a job in the real world.

We need to expand the notion of what constitutes an education after high school to include more on-the-job training, internships, and apprenticeships. By extending our definition of higher education, more attention needs to be given to "middle jobs." These are positions that do not require a bachelor's degree but pay middle-class wages. Nearly half of the jobs in the United States today that put people in the middle class are these middle jobs.

Every business owner / employer I have talked to since the mid-90s continues to say the same thing, frustrated with job openings they can't fill with qualified workers. Not only do they not have the basic skills to perform the job, but most are unable to even conduct themselves properly in a business setting. Many companies have a policy that they are always hiring, regardless of the economy, consistently looking for qualified skilled trades.

Think about it… Take an average mid-sized construction company for example. A company like this may employ 5 executive level leaders, 10 – 15 professional managers, 10 skilled office workers, and 100 – 200 craftsmen or trades people. Of those 230 employees, 25 might be college graduates, another 5 – 10 might have associates degrees or specialized training, and the remaining 195 employees can have a high school diploma / GED / or less, with on-the-job trade skill experience.

Look at the numbers… The average company is made up of 10% college degrees, 15% specialized diplomas, and 75% skill related employees. So why are we pushing our kids to certain unemployment, debt, and misery with college educations? Instead, guarantee your kids steady and rewarding employment with a trade skill.

Think it through:

"Everyone can survive without a lawyer… But no one can survive without a plumber."

Corporate executives worry more about filling these positions than they do about finding employees for high-end careers in engineering, design, and technology. Business executives state that "We can secure all the grads we need from elite schools. That's not the challenge. It's the other half of the workforce that I worry about."

As a result, some companies are taking it upon themselves to educate their own workers, bypassing the higher education system completely. Several companies actually have full-time trainers on staff and train their own employees to provide services ranging from software development to telecommunications technology, to heating and air conditioning repair. They encourage people from all walks of life who didn't go to college, because they weren't encouraged to or couldn't afford it, to come to work, and learn a skill on the job while working.

These companies are looking for that underemployed worker. The worker with good work ethic, a desire to learn, a desire to better their lives, and an aptitude for accomplishment. The average starting salary at these companies is $40,000 - $80,000. A solid wage at a time when good jobs are few and far between.

Our workforce society has become a society of managers, with no one to manage. For America to compete in the new global market, we must shift back to a society of doers, builders, creators, and entrepreneurs. We must return to what made this country strong. We didn't become a world leader by managing outsourcing to other countries. We became a world leader by outperforming other countries... And that is the only way we will rebuild our economy, our communities, our society, and this country.

CHAPTER FOUR

The Death of Craftsmanship

In Aisle 31 is precut vinyl flooring, the glue already in place, just peel and stick. In Aisle 4 are prefab doors that clip in place without using tools. Isle 10... you guessed it, a pre-assembled work bench you just haul home, so you can build your projects. Stacked 15 high near the checkout counters, and as colorful as a pre-school toy is a not-so-serious-looking power tool: a battery-operated saw-and-drill combo. And if you don't want to be your own handyman, head to Aisle 23 or Aisle 35, where a help desk will arrange for an installer. But in the checkout isle you can throw in that impulse birdhouse in a bag that requires no cutting, tools, or measuring... Just snap it together.

It's all great ideas, and convenient as hell, I guess, a convenient way to be a do-it-yourselfer without knowing the first thing about doing it yourself. But at a time when the American factory seems to be a shrinking presence, and when good manufacturing jobs have vanished, perhaps never to return, there is something deeply troubling about this dilution of American craftsmanship.

Hosting the TV show Working Class has opened my eyes even wider to the vast world of trades, vocational training, and craftsmanship that the world seems to have gone blind to. I have had the pleasure of meeting and working with some of the finest people you would ever care to meet. Learning their trades, their stories, and their journeys of how they got to where they are today. It truly saddens me to see the art of craftsmanship slowly fading into obscurity.

Is it a craftsman issue? Is it a trade issue? Is it a training issue? No… It's a social and cultural issue, as well as an economic one. The bulk home store approach to craftsmanship is to simplify it, dumb it down, and hire a contractor. It's one more sign that using tools and working with one's hands is declining in America as a hobby, as a valued skill, as a cultural influence that shaped thinking and behavior in massive sections of the country.

So where have all the craftsmen gone?… Not so very long ago, this country used to build things, and when they broke, we fixed them. In the almighty quest for efficiency, speed, and profit, we seem to have lost our craftsmen. I remember, years ago, if you wanted to build a house, the homebuilder was a craftsman that built the house from start to finish and put some pride in it. Now, if you build a house, you hire a construction manager, that subcontracts each skilled trade out to assembly line style low bid contractors. There is no pride in that.

Everyone I knew growing up, knew how to use tools. Tools were second nature, and everyone had them. Today, I would be surprised if 10% of the people in this country knew the difference between a torque wrench and a ratchet.

Can someone tell me what happened to shop class? Except in a few areas of the Midwest, shop class has ceased to exist in our school system. As a builder, I don't honestly think I would have ever gotten through projects without the solid physical foundation that I received with four years of shop class, and four years of vocational agriculture education. In high school, I learned welding, fabrication, wood working, hydraulics, small engine repair, fluid dynamics, construction, tool safety, cryogenics, and hundreds of other things that are just second nature to me now.

There is a book called "Shop Class as Soul craft" by Matthew B. Crawford. He takes this topic of what ever happened to this country's creative spirit and expounds on it. He hits it on the head, talking about the craft of fixing things, and the deeper meaning of fixing things. Sure, it is easy to throw things away, and replace them. But there is no soul in that. If you tear it apart and make it work again, you put a part of your soul, a piece of you into it. To be able to take an object, and put a piece of you into it, is a pretty special thing.

It is hard for a father to sit his son down and teach him something he can do with his hands, when we live in a disposable world. No memories of working on the car together, building a tree house, a bird house, or doghouse… It's just faster and cheaper to go buy it. There is something special about creating something… It's bigger that the object but creating memories at the same time. It's Soulful… And it saddens me that our society has become so very soulless…

It is up to us, as a society to reject what we are becoming, and put some soul back into it. We are losing our sense of community, our sense of identity, and our creativity. We need to become mentors, not only to the next generation, but to our society as a whole. I understand that technology has created a disposable world, and many things are simply not reparable, as they are designed to be replaced. But that is not the point. The point is to create something – anything in our society today that we can put our soul into…

Ask the academics why America needs more manufacturing, and they respond that manufacturing spawn's innovation, brings down the trade deficit, strengthens the dollar, generates jobs, arms the military and feeds economic growth. But rarely, if ever, do they publicly take the argument a step further, asserting that a growing manufacturing sector encourages craftsmanship and that craftsmanship is, if not a birthright, then a vital ingredient of the American self-image as a can-do, inventive, we-can-make-anything people.

That self-image is deteriorating. And the symptoms go far beyond the home do it yourselfer, that can't even assemble a pre-engineered desk in a box, armed with nothing more than a bubble wrapped Allen wrench. No one watches such classic shows like "This Old House" any more… I grew up watching it as a kid and get excited when I can find an episode now.

Traditional vocational training in public high schools is gradually declining, stranding thousands of young people who seek training for a craft without going to college. And worse, the decline in these programs fail to introduce the thousands of kids who don't even know that they have an interest in the trades of crafts. What's more, Colleges, have since 1985 graduated fewer chemical, mechanical, industrial and metallurgical engineers, partly in response to the reduced role of manufacturing, a big employer of them.

When I graduated high school, I wanted to enroll in the local vocational school for welding, but they could not offer the course that year, because there were not enough kids that wanted to enroll. So my second choice was tool and die technology. Yup, you guessed it... Not enough interest to offer that either. But there was a waiting list to get into the business management program.

The decline started as far back as the 1950s, when manufacturing generated a substantial 28 percent of the national income, or gross domestic product as we call it now, and employed one-third of the total work force. Today, factory output generates just 12 percent of G.D.P. and employs barely 9 percent of the nation's workers.

Massive layoffs and plant closings have drawn plenty of headlines and public debate over the years, and they still occasionally do. But the damage to skill trades, and craftsmanship, what's needed to build a complex airliner or a tractor, or for a worker to move up from assembler to machinist to supervisor, went largely ignored.

So, what's one explanation for the decline in traditional craftsmanship? When did the blue-collar class become the lower class in this country? Was it a lack of interest in the crafts? The big money is in fields like finance, starting in the 1980s grew in stature, and as depicted in the news media and the movies, became a more appealing source of income. It was the lure of apparently doing nothing for huge paydays. It's the same reason why so few people save money today, as opposed to 50 years ago. Today, one is more likely to have a loan than a savings account.

Today, Wall Street traders, bankers and those who deal in real estate generated 21 percent of the national income, double their share in the 1950s. And Warren E. Buffett, the good-natured financier from Nebraska, became a homespun folk hero, without the tools and overalls.

Manufacturing's shrinking presence undoubtedly helps explain the decline in craftsmanship, if only because many of the nation's assembly line workers were skilled in craft work, if not on the job, then in their spare time. The vast majority of people who work with their hands, and know a craft, will, in their off-hours, do home renovation and other skilled work. I have often thought that these extracurricular jobs were an effort on the part of the workers to regain their dignity after suffering the degradation of repetitive assembly line work in the factory. It's their way of unwinding, to grab a few beers, and pop the hood on the car, or build a new deck.

Craft work has higher status in nations like Germany, which invests in apprenticeship programs for high school students. Corporations in Germany recognized that there was an interest to be served economically and patriotically in building up a skilled labor force at home. The damage to American craftsmanship seems to parallel the quick slide in manufacturing employment. Though the decline started in the 1970s, it became much steeper beginning in 2000. Since then, some 5.3 million jobs, or one-third of the work force in manufacturing, have been lost.

CHAPTER FIVE

Shop Class

Shop class, once a staple of American high schools, has been nearly decimated by the digital age. High school students have little time for electives, and when they do, they often choose technology classes. Schools are selling off their circular saws to buy computer labs, and trading in their welding tools for webcams. After all, why do our kids need to know how to build a birdhouse when they can buy one at Home Depot for $9.99?

But new voices are calling for the return of shop class. In a time where most of our work is intangible, working with our hands can bring a sense of satisfaction that is lacking in our virtual lives. Even if one doesn't go into a manual trade, the ability to make and fix the utilities we need can help us live tangibly in an intellectual world. Here is a list of reasons why every student should be offered the opportunity to take shop class:

1. **Become Self-Reliant.**
   The generation before us sewed their own clothes, changed their own oil, and built their own fences. But now, what ordinary people once made, they buy, and what they once fixed for themselves, they replace entirely or hire an expert to repair. This leads to a feeling of dependence, of being unable to navigate the world on one's own. Students learn to be practical by acquiring the know-how they'll need to survive. Once they've designed and created their own step stool, they're more willing to look at a broken faucet

and think, I can fix that. This not only saves money, but helps people feel more in control of their own lives.

2. **Understand the Principals of Math and Science.**

   "Project based learning" Much of our business world has become "Project Based". Students learn better when learning grows out of an interesting project. Shop class is the original project-based laboratory. Students must learn math and physics if their projects are to succeed. The Pythagorean Theorem, fractions, and geometry all come to life when it's time to build an octagonal end table.

3. **Learn the Value of Persistence.**

   Most classes in school emphasize getting the right answer the first time. Our current educational process is based on being given the correct answer, and then being expected to regurgitate that answer sometime in the future. Students become fearful of doing things the wrong way and may become discouraged about trying at all. The system leaves no room for learning because you never learn anything by doing it right. You learn by making mistakes and leaning from those mistakes. But in shop class, persistence is encouraged. There's more than one way to get something done. And if something goes wrong, it can be undone and fixed. Shop class teaches our children to persevere, to look beyond the first failure and keep trying until they succeed.

4. **Find Satisfaction in Taking a Project from Start to Finish.**

   Initiative and hard work are far more critical to success than intelligence. Intelligence has virtually no impact on one's success. Success is derived from tenacity, luck, determination, and a love of what you do. Shop class is one of the few places where students are encouraged to envision a project and then figure out a plan to make it happen. There is no better way to stimulate creativity and problem-solving than to allow a student free reign with a room full of power tools, doing work that fully engages his mind and his body. They'll never forget the satisfaction of pointing to a project and saying, "I made that."

5. **Help Students Find Their Strengths.**

   Not every student finds school easy. It is an institution that emphasizes intellectual ability over all other talents. Shop class is one of the few places where students are encouraged to explore other skills. It is important for our children to experience a variety of opportunities in school. That's how they can determine at what they can be successful. Once a child feels capable in one area, his confidence will carry over to the rest of his activities.

6. **Launch a Hands-on Career.**

Our country works because we have all kinds of different people doing a variety of work. We do need engineers and lawyers, but we also need skilled electricians and plumbers. Job satisfaction in these trades is good because, there's nothing like taking an idea, a concept, and turning it into a tangible thing. Additionally, these jobs offer security because they cannot be out-sourced or off-shored.

If we are going to make a resurgence in shop classes, then we must be relevant. We can't just bring back wood shop, building cutting boards, and bird houses. We need to do those things, but also embrace the technology that is a part of everyday blue-collar work.

Vocational students in today's auto-body shop, don't just learn how to change oil or hammer out a dent. They use computer diagnostic equipment to fix cars and learn the green technologies of hybrid vehicles and hydrogen fuel cells. For kids in welding classes, a water-jet cutter not only represents the latest in high tech cutting equipment, using high water pressure to quickly slice through metal, it also teaches the math needed to program the machine. And in construction classes, students still build in between lessons on résumé creation and proper work-site communication.

Welcome to the 21st-century shop class. In pockets around the country, a retooling of classes in career and technical education aims to give students job training, exposure to new technologies, and windows into different careers. The resurgence of shop has been slowly taking place nationwide over the last several years, partly in a response to industry demand. When shop classes began a decline in the 1970s, coinciding with a push toward college-bound classes, so did the number of young people entering skilled trades. Now, industries facing a worker shortage are pushing for the classes' return.

It's not your father's shop class. The new incarnations of shop are a far cry from the old, in large part because technology has evolved so much. Today's classes incorporate a range of those abilities widely promoted as 21st-century skills, involving technology, communication, and collaboration.

You only must look to many schools now collaborating with car manufacturers. Students learn to use a diagnostic system to check a car's computer systems in their automotive program. In today's auto-shop classes, teachers create a problem somewhere in a car, or in special stand-alone training units that represent a car, and students must figure out what's wrong. It teaches them today's automotive technology, as well as critical-thinking skills and teamwork.

In some schools' design and drafting and machine shop classes, students use a computer-assisted-design program called SolidWorks, in which they can create three-dimensional drawings. And the welding program's water-jet cutter (besides adding a cool factor for students who've seen one on the television shows) requires users to plot out the settings on a computer graph.

Of course, they also prepare students for jobs. The need for trained technical workers didn't go away when shop classes dropped out of vogue. In fact, it is rising, according to the latest job-outlook report from the U.S. Bureau of Labor Statistics. It predicts, for example, that there will be more machinist jobs than skilled workers available over the next seven years. And employers say they already have a hard time finding adequately skilled auto technicians and mechanics jobs expected to increase by about 10,000 a year.

Some schools are developing building-trades programs to give his students a range of skills they'll need on the job. In addition to classroom instruction, students design and build a house from start to finish that is then auctioned off at the end of the year. By doing this, it teaches students the business of home building, and then follows up with soft skills, such as appropriate communication on the job and how to create a résumé. And because the house is then auctioned off, there is no impact to the school's budget... A very creative and innovative solution to providing real world experience to the students, while overcoming administrative and budgetary constraints.

The economy really is what drives the idea of career programs. We as a society need to get off this idea, we put into our kid's heads of going to Harvard and landing that six-figure job out of college. It is not reality. Yes, we all want better for our kids, but if you are generation "X" or later, I'm pretty sure you didn't have it too bad, and maybe it wouldn't be so bad if our kids had to struggle a little bit, and work for what they want.

Nevertheless, today's shop classes, like the multitude of other career and technical education classes offered around the country, also emphasize the postsecondary education option. The programs can push students into apprenticeships or certification programs or offer college credit. Teachers need to develop materials that show how students can continue their education, based on what career classes they take, after high school. There are many programs that offer college credit through either two-year or four-year colleges.

But whether students are looking for serious job training or a curriculum-enhancing elective, these hands-on classes offer them something we all need: life skills. You're going to own a house at some point in time, and the stuff shop class teaches you is something you can use.

CHAPTER SIX

The Significance of Craftsmanship

There are many ideas concerning what is meant by the concept of craftsmanship. It has been said that craftsmanship is what makes a product have the immediate appeal of being well made and well-functioning at its very early interactions with the customer. In other words, a product that is well crafted is one that, right from the start, comes across as being carefully designed, produced, and in addition there are no initial reasons to doubt the ability of the product to do its job well. It has also been said that the idea of craftsmanship is creating products that are skillfully created, lasting in nature and possessing a timeless elegance. In this way, attention to detail, material selection, careful workmanship and innovative product design are all key components.

Concerning products that are mass produced, industry has developed standards of quality in an attempt to give their products this sense of craftsmanship. From the definitions given above, and others however, it seems that craftsmanship goes beyond simple quality. Consider that the precise use of good machinery can produce many different products with perfect quality. What is it then that sets these technically 'good' products apart from those that are deemed to be well crafted? It would seem that there must be something in the attention that is given to detail.

Many products that are mass produced are simply designed such that they are easy to form. A product that is carefully designed and takes time and skill to produce requires extra attention and is thus more one-of-a-kind. Products that are carefully produced have also traditionally shown less inclination to fall apart or not work properly. Overall, then one can infer that a product, even one produced on large scale, might be considered well-crafted only if serious attention to detail is given in both design and production.

Craftsmanship is finishing each step of your project, such as removing glue squeeze-out, hiding nail holes with wood putty and sanding, straight lines on all cuts, radius cuts free of flat spots, paint-stains applied evenly, sanding is paramount to a fine finish, Craftsmen have steps they go thru when doing a project, and they finish each step before moving to the next step.

They use exact measurements, and exact cut. When you have 4 boards that need to be cut 9 - 3/8" long and 6 – 1/4" wide, a beginner might cut a board 9 - 3/8" and then change the fence setting to cut the 6 - 1/4" side, the problem here is when you go back to cut the other boards at the 9 - 3/8" you can be off a fraction and then the fit becomes ill fitting, and assembly problematic. A craftsmen would cut all the boards at the 9 - 3/8" length and then cut the 6 - 1/4" wide side, each length dimension being the same, and each width dimension the same. I know this explanation refers working in wood, BUT, apply these principles to any craft you're working on, it works. Planning, patience, accuracy, finishing each step & finish the finish. "CLOSE ENOUGH" Is not a Craftsman!

Historically, we only need to look to China for a real appreciation of the craftsman. In China, rural life was the major lifestyle, as most aspired to live rurally, rather than in cities. From the earliest ages of civilizations in China, craftsmen held the significant position in the social structure. They devoted their lives to their craft and served the community. Even though farmers played an important role for survival of the community, the appreciation of the craftsmen had more significance. Farmers only followed the procedures to cultivate crops to avoid hunger; in contrast, craftsmen had to not merely satisfy people's needs on various material for storage, for cooking, for drinking, etc., but also focus on immaterial needs for culture, information, ideas, emotion, stories, etc. Thus, traditional construction and beautification of ceramics had been developed and evolved alongside each other.

I believe, in our modern consuming society, most purchasers of a Chinese 18th Century porcelain vase should care more about the story behind this vase, the construction, the craftsmanship, instead of what kind of flowers they should put in it. They should not simply appreciate the elegant appearance of the vase, but also the sophisticated skill of craftsmen that created it.

In other words, this vase is not just vase. If one listens, it speaks to us. It expresses the human struggle, and the traditional expression. Most people are not even aware of the craftsmanship in the vase. They just see a vase, and it either appeals to them, or is does not, based solely on their taste, and the physical appearance of the vase. When I see things, I not only see the physical appearance of the items, but I look deeper in the craftsmanship of how it was built, and what tools may have been available at the time. Our craftsmen define our society, today, just as they have defined their societies for thousands of years.

They don't make them like they used to… How many times have you heard that? How many times have you stopped and reflected on it? It's an embarrassing testament to what we have become. We don't care enough about our society, our communities, our legacy, or ourselves to take the time to produce something that will be on this earth long after we are not. I know it sounds corny, and maybe I'm just an old soul, but I want to leave something tangible on this earth past my days here. I want to leave something that someone will cherish, and treasure. Whether it be a handmade oak desk, a fine crafted cabinet, a painting, a building, a piece of artwork, or whatever interests you enough to take the time to pour a part of your soul into creating it.

So why does any of this matter? With the advance of the industrial age and the subsequent emergence of the knowledge economy, the crafts have become disregarded in the economy, and looked down upon by society as a whole. Traditional crafts were just that, traditional, and something that your grandparents did for a living, and only interesting as part of cultural heritage. People seem to think that utilitarian crafts like plumbers, housepainters, roof workers, carpenters, welders, electricians and so on, are low-class blue-collar trades. And who wants to be that loser who went to vocational school, and comes to my house to fix my toilet?

Well, if we didn't live in a society that has become filled with such arrogance, we might understand the economics of it. So, let's educate the college graduate for a moment.

> The average business school graduate with a 4-year bachelor degree in business graduates with $50,000 - $100,000 in school loans, makes a starting salary of about $41,000, and has zero experience to show an employer. This is a clear recipe for long term failure, because finding a job that pays the bills, and college debt is nearly impossible.

> While, on the other hand, the average union electrician graduates his apprenticeship program, which he got paid to do, with zero debt, makes a starting salary of about $44,000, and has between 2- and 4-years' experience to show his employer, making him or her a highly sought after asset.

The educational systems, in an effort to advance their own self-preservation, and arrogance look down on manual skills. In the arts, conceptual innovation has overtaken craftsmanship as the core competence. Just look at what was considered art 200 years ago, and what passes for art today. There was always a fine line between an artist, and a great craftsman, and in my opinion, they are one in the same. Today... Not so much.

Just look back at the freemason society. For hundreds of years the members of the freemason society were the elite of the elite. The founders of this

country, and some would argue the framework of all world society is the blueprint of the freemason society. Freemasons started as just that... An apprenticeship and master mason framework of builders. Yup! The tradesmen were the respected class of society, because everyone knew that without the craftsmen, society would not function.

Again, why is this important? Because the pendulum is beginning to swing the other way, and all you know about our culture is about to change. The creative economy increasingly calls for skills that are characteristic for craftsmanship. And guess what? There are very few of them out there, which means that the value of craftsmen is going through the roof. Craftsmanship is going to be required as our culture moves away from being a throwaway society. Recycling, and repairing rather than replacing, eco-responsibility are all driving the need to again craftsmen to build things that last.

Craftsmanship furthermore satisfies the need for meaningful work. Mastery provides a sense of self-worth. Politicians, therefore, are speaking about the importance of craftsmanship, and artists are reevaluating the craft in their work. Our society has created an economy of unfulfilling jobs, that we all hate, and no one has any pride in. You are seeing more movement to small business, anti-corporations, minimalism, simplicity, and anti-consumerism. These are all trends that increase the need for craftsmanship, and pride in creating something that will outlast you. Something you can point to and say... "Yeah, I made that".

CHAPTER SEVEN

The Trade of Being a Tradesman

For many years now, the hardest segment of the workforce for employers to staff with skilled talent hasn't been registered nurses or engineers or even web developers. It's been the skilled trades… The welders, electricians, machinists, etc. that are so prevalent in manufacturing and construction.

Don't believe me? Find a good plumber. Find a good mechanic. Find a good electrician. Oh, they are out there. But the ones that are good, are busy. Once you find one, see how long it takes to get on the schedule.

Now do the math… If these skilled-trades workers are difficult to find now, just wait a few years. As all the "Old-timers" continue to retire, as the younger kids flock to college instead of to the skilled trades. If I were 18 years old, I'd be in trade school acquiring a skill, rather than a generic degree that really has no definable skill attached to it.

Definition of a college education:

> College prepares us to assimilate into a civilized society with a set of undefinable skills that help us to adapt, and learn general concepts, and apply them in such a way as to implement process and progress.

Definition of a skilled trade:

> A skilled trade prepares us to directly implement action resulting in a definable accomplishment, or final outcome that clearly provides a service.

Now think about it in this way... Let's assume for a moment that rather than continued progress, society were to actually regress. Let's assume that the impossible were to occur. People were losing their jobs, companies were closing, and people were losing their homes, cars, and life savings. Our economy were on the verge of collapse, and the stock market were to drop like a rock... Sound scary? Sound impossible?

Think again! There have been as many as 47 recessions in the United States since 1790 which these things occurred in each and every one. Cycles in agriculture, consumption, business investment, and the health of the banking industry also contribute to these declines. U.S. recessions have increasingly affected economies on a worldwide scale, especially as countries' economies become more intertwined, and it will become even more prevalent as the years go by.

Look at the COVID recession of 2020, when they shut down the entire economy. Who were the essential workers? Construction, manufacturing, nurses, etc. The skilled trades were essential. Middle managers, professionals, and typical college educated professions were not essential, and many of these people lost everything.

During these inevitable cycles of recession, the need for professional services dramatically declines, and many of these highly educated professionals lose their jobs. However, even in the middle of economic downturn, people need skilled trades. Pipes need fixed, cars need repaired, hair needs cut, and basic services carry on. If you are a skilled tradesman, even if you lose your job, you can still provide a valuable service to others by providing your skills.

Skilled trades can provide a promising career path depending on a job seeker's skills and location. However, some of these middle-skill occupations will need an influx of new talent sooner than others. There's a lot of talk about manufacturing jobs continuing to go away in this country. But for manufacturers, one of the biggest issues they talk about is finding qualified labor. Apprentice programs for tool and die makers are shrinking due to lack of interest. Even factory production jobs aren't menial labor jobs anymore. It takes skill and training to run CNC or other sophisticated machines.

The same is true with professional tradesmen in the contracting field. Talk to a plumbing or electrical contractor and they say the same thing. There aren't enough young folks getting into those trades as well.

So, what's the problem? A good plumber or electrician can make a very good living and their jobs can't be outsourced. Spokespeople like Mike Rowe has a passion to get more people into the trades. He's even testified in Washington about the challenges that face us as a nation.

The same holds true in the manufacturing sector. There are good jobs for those that are trained properly. I know Skills for America's Future and the Manufacturing Institute are trying to work with community colleges to develop successful programs so young folks can enter the workforce with skill sets necessary to get and keep a good job. Even politicians are endorsing a manufacturing skills credentialing system and I hope it's going to be more than window dressing.

While this country has been transitioning to a "knowledge economy", not all is lost. No matter how smart we think we are, the economic and cultural shift is create new trades that may become more attractive to younger people. The nice thing about working in the trades is that as technology moves forward, we create new trade sectors.

However, the fastest-growing jobs in America are not the "knowledge economy" jobs we usually think of. In fact, the rising importance of the healthcare sector to the economy and the transition of the economy to services, where "services" is not a synonym for "computers" but, like, actual services, is going to shift more emphasis on trades and vocational training. For example, A "Diagnostic Medical Sonographer" is a highly skilled job that doesn't require college training in the sense that you can learn everything you need to do the job in a manner of months. Another growing sector is "In-Home Health", which also does not require a four-year college degree. Not all trades jobs are in plumbing and carpentry.

The problem, in my opinion, is perception by young people that those kinds of jobs aren't cool, and they are low paying. Also, most guidance counselors with most high schools are pointing everyone to college. Not everyone is 4-year college material. What young people don't realize is that a plumber or journeyman electrician makes more than 4-year college graduates and they don't have all those student loans to pay off.

Our challenge as an industry is to somehow mount a campaign to kids at an early age to show them that these kinds of jobs are cool and just as important, if not more so, than someone sitting behind a desk. Ideally, trade and manufacturing associations should come together and mount a public service campaign. Someone must take the first step and we need someone visible enough to carry the message and credibility to the young folks.

CHAPTER EIGHT

A Cultural Shift

So how did this country go from overcoming the settling of a new land, beating the odds of survival, enduring revolutionary war, surviving two world wars, and industrial revolution, ending the cold war, and becoming the world's undisputed super-power, to the bankrupt, jobless shell of a country imploding upon itself a little more each day? Don't misunderstand... I love America. I love our tenacity, our over the top, in your face enthusiasm for being the biggest, and best at everything. I love that the rest of the world hates us, because they all want to be us.

But really?... What happened to this country? We got too smart for our own good, which then led to us becoming lazy, breeding an entitlement mentality. We went from a country of producers to a country of managers.

Back in the 1960s, the hippie generation decided that instead of learning a trade and working for a living, it would be better if we all became academics, and instead of outworking the rest of the world, as we had for the last 200 years. We decided that we could simply become smarter than everyone else, let them do the work, and we would just manage the process, and think up new things... And we would call it outsourcing.

Outsourcing is the practice of relocating certain production type jobs from abroad, where wages are lower and other conditions are favorable because they lower a company's overhead. Outsourcing typically involves the reallocation of menial/labor-oriented jobs, often production tasks, to another country, while administrative operations remain centralized in the U.S. These countries are chosen as sites for outsourcing because they offer a number of attractive and competitive benefits. Labor laws, wage laws, and tax laws all create favorable conditions that help a company lower its overhead and increase its profit. Outsourcing in the United States began taking ahold in the 1970s and has become increasingly popular, particularly with the explosion of globalization.

As founding companies began experiencing success with outsourcing in terms of the economy and their businesses, other industries and businesses began to establish operational branches abroad. The core industries that currently utilize outsourcing include phone-based customer service relations, production of material goods such as clothing, shoes, and car parts, and accounting.

What those 1960s hippies never thought of was that by trading vocational skills for academic skills, we as a country, become completely dependent on other countries. We have lost the ability to compete with other counties known for their ability to produce. Menial and technological jobs that are outsourced contribute to unemployment among those who cannot take the college path, while foreign students who come here to earn for degrees are returning to their home countries and implementing the business side of the equation thereby eliminating any need for us Americans to manage and think of new things.

Companies that use outsourcing insist that there are many benefits that make outsourcing preferable to the centralization of business within the U.S and lowers a company's overhead because it transfers operations to countries where operational costs tend to be lower. This benefit is passed on directly to the consumer, who enjoys lower prices and thus has minimal incentive to complain about outsourcing unless it affects his or her community directly in terms of job loss. Outsourcing benefits other countries' economies as well, and it is not infrequent to see proponents of outsourcing lauding the fact that this practice results in productive employment for people living in economically and professionally depressed areas. Outsourcing provides workers in other countries with a higher wage than they might receive normally, and it relieves the burden of another country's government to provide jobs for its workers.

While other countries are benefitting, Americans simply cannot produce enough professional jobs for everyone. We have become a nation of managers with nothing to manage. This leads to a reduction in the quality of life. Without a job, you experience such problems as spiraling personal debt, the loss of one's car or home, and the inability to pay for a child's education, thus perpetuating the cycle of economic and vocational poverty. These are indirect but important economic impacts of outsourcing.

Finally, another negative outcome of outsourcing is that jobs in certain sectors, especially technology, effectively lure foreign nationals educated in the U.S. back to their home countries, causing the United States to experience a phenomenon known as exporting our educational advantage. After offering generous scholarships, grants, and in-kind support to foreign nationals, increasing numbers of U.S. educated foreigners are returning to their home countries to pursue lucrative job opportunities offered by United States companies. In many cases, foreign nationals may already have initiated the visa process that would allow them to remain in the United States to work, but their return to the home country aborts that process, resulting in unnecessary costs that cannot be recuperated by U.S. based employers.

How could we let this happen? This country managed to take hundreds of years of vocational training tradition, and a century of industrial revolution leading to world industrial dominance and throw it away in a few decades. I'll tell you how… **Educated idiots…**

This is a term that means a lot of different things to a lot of different people. You know who I am talking about. The guy with a PHD in physics but can't change a tire on his car. The guy who has an MBA but can't balance his own checkbook. The guy with a bachelor's degree in finance but filed for bankruptcy last year. Yeah, they are the educated idiots, but it goes even further than that.

How about the ones who can't do simple math without a calculator? But I take it a step further. In order to retain your man card, you should be able to change a tire, read a tape measure, use a hand saw, hammer a 16-penny nail in 4 hits without missing or bending the nail, and have a basic understanding of the internal combustion engine. Better yet, hand a non-digital clock to a 15-year-old, and ask them what time it is… Good luck getting an answer.

We are living in an age of the "enlightenment" set into motion by the educated, all started by the "Hippie" generation that brought you outsourcing. They all know better how to raise our kids, shape society, and implement our values.

The 1950s was the last age of innocence. Families sat together to eat dinner and kids said the Pledge of Allegiance in school. You had homework and chores to do and if you disrespected a teacher or an adult neighbor you were grounded or severely punished. Spankings were part of life, and there was zero tolerance for misbehaving. Kids were safe and could walk the streets in the evening without fear of being accosted or abducted. Parents didn't have to worry about their children's safety as much as they do today. When teens needed money, they worked in burger joints or as babysitters.

Kids didn't sit in front of the TV, and there were no computers. Kids were either outside playing (using their imagination) or were out with their groups of friends hanging out at their favorite cafe. Our music was even better than today. The songs were either love songs or happy songs. It wasn't depressing.

When your parents said "NO" it meant just that! They knew that if they loved you, protected you, put a roof over your head, food in your stomach, gave you an education and quality time then you had nothing to complain about. But you had to keep your own room clean, wash/dry and iron your own clothes, help cook meals, mow lawns or shovel snow. Today if you asked a teen to mow your lawn or shovel snow, they'd look at you like you were crazy! Girls babysat from the age of 12 on, to help pay for their school clothes.

Nick Kasik

By the time you were 17 years old, you had your life together, because you knew that at age 18, you had three choices. Get a job, join the military, or go to college. Those were your only three choices, and if your parents weren't wealthy, you only had two choices... And it was okay.

Today... young people are directionless, sitting on the couch playing video games all day, and nothing seems to be important to them anymore. They have no goals, no real hopes or dreams, and no plan. Half of them stay with their parents until well into their twenties because no one gave them any hope that they could go out and make it.

It's almost as if society has forced kids to give up. Culture convinced them that life was easy, and they should expect to have a 5,000 square foot house on the beach, a BMW, and money to go clubbing every night with no education or job.

CHAPTER NINE

Skilled Trades vs. College Degrees

T rade School or College… But, what's best for me?

Many believe that attending a four-year college is a necessary for career success. But the reality is that many students are entering college after high school completely unprepared – academically, emotionally, and financially.

Tens of thousands of dollars are spent on four-year universities by students who are not 100% sure why they are going. As a result, students often struggle to pay back loans with no job to support them. How many kids are two or three years into college, and still have not picked a major? Or worse yet, settle for a major, because they simply don't know what to do.

The irony is that there are many job options more readily available to graduates, including work in skilled trades. Many of these jobs may be obtained faster and easier than jobs from a four-year college, if you get the right credentials.

A common argument for getting a bachelor's degree is higher lifetime earnings over someone who only has a high school degree. While statistics on the future of our workforce challenges this argument. A lot of those who have low lifetime earnings may not have necessarily benefited from college. For many people, college is simply not the best place to learn how to earn a living, and that's okay!

For others, they thrive in an academic atmosphere. If you have aspirations to be a doctor, lawyer, or Professor, then college is going to be your best path to success and ultimate happiness. If you are an intellectual type of person who achieves happiness as a researcher, or academic professional, that's great. College is the path for you.

The problem comes from the masses of students who enter a four-year college with no clue what to study, not because they have a passion for the academics, but because they have no clue what else to do, they don't want to flip burgers forever, and because their parents made them go to college.

Even once a four-year degree has been earned, eligible career paths and starting yearly salary depends on the major. A good two-year degree or diploma can pay better than many four-year degrees.

For decades, a college degree spoke for itself. A diploma meant you were one of the lucky few who had the brains, strength, or bank account to earn an education which, in turn, made you an exceptional, marketable asset to many employers. But, when the supply of college graduates increased, the value of that diploma decreased, and the diploma was degraded. It's a matter of pure economics.

That's, partly, the reason why a new premium has been placed on advanced degrees. With a bachelor's degree in the 1980s, one could easily secure an entry level professional position. However, by the 2000s, applicants for these same entry-level positions were not even considered unless they held a master's degree. You want to show employers you're really worth hiring, forget the undergrad, where's that masters?

In 2020, the annual salary for an English or Sociology major averaged out at about $42,000. The average four-year bill for college will run you about $100,000. That is excluding the fact you may want to live a little or keep a roof over your head.

And no one is guaranteed to graduate in only four years, as six-year graduations are becoming increasingly common among both non-competitive and highly competitive schools.

For example, employers in the stereotypically "blue collar" manufacturing industry need skilled workers. And as demand for these skilled workers increases, so too does compensation. Again, with the basic economics! A 2020 salary survey found that manufacturing employees earned an average salary of $65,000 annually, while the median college graduate salary wage was $52,000.

When you consider this, it's puzzling to think that so many "educated" young 20-somethings living in their parents' basements, holding out for a career that is "fulfilling." Many factors are at play, but it's hard not to wonder whether the cultural emphasis on the college credential has led to a degradation of skilled labor. But I still must ask, is being unemployed, but with a degree, really that much more noble than working in a factory without one?

Due to these reasons, enrollment in a trade school can be a better option for many middle-class students than going straight to college after high school. Another option would be to enroll in a two-year college to "find yourself" and get your general studies out of the way at a lower cost, and then transfer to a four year college once you know what you want to get your degree in. Yet another option is to go to school to pick up a specific trade, as many only take as short as 6-10 weeks on average, and work in that trade to fund your four-year college degree.

I must fault many high school counselors and administrative managers because they really don't promote the trades as a viable, noble option to most students. I graduated high school in a predominantly blue-collar area, where I would estimate 80% of the community was blue collar, and still, my high school counselor largely dismissed me, simply because I was not interested in a four-year degree. School administrators are obviously a product of a four-year degree, so they are largely biased to the four-year institutions, unintentionally dismissing those who lean toward the trades.

How many times have you seen a high school guidance counselor actually promote the opportunities of the local plumber's union, and help kids understand and enroll in the apprenticeship training programs? It largely just doesn't happen.

Here is another little secret... As a general rule, most "professional" careers, which are generally the management jobs with bachelor's degrees, require 50-60 hours a week, and pay an annual salary that does not take into account the hours you may be forced to work. They are based on a 40-hour week.

Conversely, skilled trades are virtually always paid on an hourly rate. You get paid based on the hours you work, and if you go over that 40 hour a week threshold, not only will you get paid, but you will generally be compensated 1.5 times your hourly rate.

As you can see below how the academic four-year college majors and average salaries stack up. However, note that the jobs they are getting are probably not the ones they wanted. Statistically, nearly 40 percent of working recent graduates are in jobs that do not require a college degree."

College Degree Starting Salaries

Business	$40,446
Communications	$41,367
Computer Sciences	$59,234
Education	$38,461
Engineering	$59,496
Health Sciences	$45,903
Humanities/Social Sciences	$36,319
Math & Sciences	$42,002

Conversely, the jobs and average salaries for skilled trades jobs requiring 2 years or less formal education are far more varied, with a ton of flexibility, variety, and financial flexibility.

Trade Starting Salaries

Instrument Technician	$59,500
Electrician	$76,400
Heavy Equipment Operator	$68,500
Welding Journeyman	$55,900
Millwright	$63,600
CAD Drafter	$57,000
Heavy Mechanic	$56,000
Machinist	$52,500
Plumber	$76,500
Brick mason	$67,000
Carpenter	$57,500
Ironworker	$69,500
Cement Finisher	$41,000
Pipefitter	$79,900
Roofer	$39,000
Sheet Metal Journeyman	$86,600
Truck Driver	$66,900
Motorcycle Mechanic	$46,000
Facility Maintenance	$65,000
Lineman	$75,600
Aircraft Assembly Tech.	$79,200
CNA	$39,000
Dental Assistant	$43,600
Diesel Mechanic	$57,500
Auto Mechanic	$53,000
Carpet Installer	$44,400
Payroll Administrator	$51,000
Barber	$40,000
Correctional Officer	$55,000
Insurance Appraiser	$56,000
Loan Officer	$66,400

Purchasing Agent	$56,600
Investigator	$58,000
Construction Field Supervisor	$68,700
Refinery Operator	$69,000
Postmaster	$60,300
Camera man	$62,600
Sonographer	$64,400
Nurse	$65,000
Commercial Pilot	$77,000
Firefighter	$68,000
Dental Hygienist	$68,500
Nuclear Med Tech.	$68,700
Detective	$68,800
Sales – nonretail	$89,000
Elevator Technician	$70,900
Power Plant Operator	$85,700
Municipal Admin Supervisor	$77,900
Radiation Therapist	$74,800
Police Admin Supervisor	$78,200
Transport / Distribution Mgr.	$80,200
Field Construction Manager	$83,300
General Operations Manager	$94,400
Air Traffic Controller	$108,000

The fact is, there is a place in society for everyone. Much has been written about the lack of discipline in kids who skate by on "C"s and "D"s, skip classes and eventually drop out. As the cynics keep telling us, nothing can be done with these lazy, low-achieving slackers because the root causes are broken homes and lousy parenting.

Yet, in my experience, when you offer these same kids the right form of education for them, they flourish. The magic of learning something that is useful and relevant sparks a strong desire to achieve. The transformative power of education is considerable. These kids are not necessarily the losers who cannot be taught, or who cannot conform, they may simply not be interested in what society has had to offer them to this point.

Let's face it. I was one of those kids who skated by on straight "C"s, not because I was stupid... Quite the opposite, I was smart enough to pay no attention, do no work, and show up for the tests, and still pass, while the brainiacs were spending all their time and effort cramming to get "A"s and "B"s, which, in the end made no difference because we both got the same diploma. I had no desire to get an "A", because I had no desire to get into college. I just wanted to develop a craft, work a fulfilling job, and be happy... And there are a lot of people just like me out there...

CHAPTER TEN

Feed your Soul

We live in a harsh and stressful world, and sometimes we need to have that outlet to feed our soul. To bring back some compassion and purpose of something other than business, survival, paying the bills and all the things that go along with life as we know it.

I have worked in both worlds. I have strapped on a tool belt, went out and worked with my hands. Sweat, dirt, and calluses don't scare me. And on the other hand, I have worked in jobs that tied me into the office all day, never to see anyone or anything going on around me. Honestly, they both have their ups and downs.

But after all that, you need to feed your soul. You need to do something that you enjoy. Something that is not work to you, even though it might be very hard work. For me... It is welding. I can go into the shop, and start building something, and when that welding hood goes down, all time stops. It's dirty, smoky, smelly, and not very healthy, you cut your hands, and occasionally take a spark down the back, or drop a piece of slag down your shoe. Heck I've even caught my own jeans on fire more than once while I was welding. But who cares?! Not me. I forget everything, and just create. I become immersed in the craft, and only focus on doing the craft well. I lose track of time, and I feed my soul. Now imagine doing something like that every day. Imagine doing something like that for your job. It makes your current mind-numbing office puke job seem pretty lame, doesn't it?

Your craft is part sweat, drudgery, and sometimes danger. And the craft is the joy, the fulfillment, the pride, and the essence of growth. Our work produces results that we can see, measure, and hold up as a testament to what we do. But the results are not the same as the work that produced them. They reflect a job well done, or perhaps not so well done. Some results, whether they are intangible or a hard-edged product, have more quality than others. Craftsmanship describes high-quality work that produces high-quality results.

Many folks who might describe themselves as craftsmen like carpenters, plumbers, electricians may not actually be craftsmen at all. They may just be tradesmen... There is a difference. A true craftsmanship is the quintessence of quality. There are still pockets of craftsmanship. They tend to cluster where there is variability in the raw materials of work. Things that are not well done by machine are the things best done by application of intellect and touch. Woodworking is an example. Although it is subjected to machine work and shaped by it, the best woodwork still demands a craftsman. Wood is complex and variable. It requires adjustment and accommodation, precisely the kind of things those human beings are good at. When raw materials get variable and complex, automation won't always cut it. Somebody has to care enough to do it right and do it better. At its heart, craftsmanship is about caring about the outcome, having pride in not only the outcome, but also the work itself, and feeding their soul simply for the love of their craft.

Another way that the craftsmanship can feed your soul is through passing that craft on to a person who has an interest in getting more out of their job than a paycheck. Any one of us are capable of earning a paycheck if we so desire. And yes, earning that paycheck has a sense of accomplishment in earning the means to feed your family and provide for others. But pride in your craft, and a sense of accomplishment are two very different things.

A sense of accomplishment can come from the simplest of tasks like taking out the trash or doing the laundry. But there is no pride in that. There is no feeding of the soul in that. Compare the feeling to showing your grandfather the hand carved oak desk that you spent 6 months building, or the portrait that you painted. There is a difference, and as subtle as it may be, it makes all the difference in the world.

Another way to feed your soul is to pass that craft on to the next generation. Teach your children, not only the trade, and the skills of the craft, but also the soul of the craft. The essence of the history, and tradition of the craft. Do some research, and find out more about the craft, because a true craftsman will know the history of his craft. Create a tradition, even if only as a hobby.

This craftsmanship crisis has been building for decades or more now. So much human potential is squandered, so much time spent grinding one's wheels can exhaust one's fuel for living. So what happens now? More of the same?

Not a chance. What happens now is this. We create the future.

We're on the cusp of what I call The Living Age. An age in history rich with ideas about, and great transformations. Life lived meaningfully well. We hold the chance to shift the thinking in this country away from consumerism, toward living well. Living complete. Living simpler.

We have grown to hate our jobs. Hate Mondays. Hate our co-workers. Hate our bosses. Hate what we do. Hate the fact that we are so far in debt that we have no choice but to continue. Hate the never-ending trap that is our life.

We have a chance to take our lives back, and in turn take this country back. What if... Think for a moment... What if we all loved our job? What if we all had a job where we produced something that we loved to produce, and others appreciated it as much as we did? What if there was a market for that product that was able to sustain you, and you could just pass the skill on to your children without having to go into debt for college? What if your job not only paid the bills, but what if you job could feed your soul?

Now get out there and find that thing. That craft that feeds your soul. Learn it. Learn everything there is to learn about it. Learn the history, the future, the concepts, the skills, the traditions, and then pass that craft on to someone else. Create a new tradition. Create something that outlives you... And that will feed your soul.

CHAPTER ELEVEN

Developing Your Character within Your Craft

To be a craftsman, it requires more than just a mastery of the craft. It also requires a mastery of the craft of character. This chapter touches on the ten points of character that every person needs to succeed. Like a set of ten fingers, you can get the job done without them all. But it will be harder and take longer than if you have all ten working together.

As you read through the ten points of character, think about how you can implement these points into your career, your work, your craft, and your life. These points transcend work to life, and back again. If you can master your craft, and take pride in your craft, you will not only have mastered the craft, but also your life.

When you properly develop your craft, you as an individual develop along with it. And when you develop in this manner you become a better person and better employee. In today's world, how many times do we hear professionals hitting a mid-life crisis wanting to find themselves, and feeling like they have missed something? Feeling like they hate their jobs. Feeling like they took a wrong turn somewhere. While at the same time, you never hear a craftsman who has mastered their craft say that same thing. Why? Because when you properly develop your craft, you develop within. You simply become a better, more complete person.

1. Strong Work Ethic

People look to others who understand and possess a willingness to work hard. In addition to working hard it is also important to work smart. This means learning the most efficient way to complete tasks and finding ways to save time while completing daily assignments. It's also important to care about your job and complete all projects while maintaining a positive attitude. Doing more than is expected on the job is a good way to show management that you utilize good time management skills and don't waste valuable company time attending to personal issues not related to the job. Downsizing in today's job market is quite common so it's important to recognize the personal values and attributes employers want to improve your chances of job security should a layoff occur.

2. Dependability and Responsibility

Be on time. People value others who are there when they are supposed to be, and are responsible for their actions and behavior. It's important to keep supervisors abreast of changes in your schedule or if you are going to be late for any reason. This also means keeping your supervisor informed on where you are on all projects you have been assigned. Being dependable and responsible as an employee shows your employer that you value your job and that you are responsible in keeping up with projects and keeping them informed of the things that they should know about.

3. Possessing a Positive Attitude.

Everyone values people who take the initiative and have the motivation to get the job done in a reasonable period of time. A positive attitude gets the work done and motivates others to do the same without dwelling on the challenges that inevitably come up in any job. It is the enthusiastic employee who creates an environment of good will and who provides a positive role model for others. A positive attitude is something that is most valued by supervisors and co-workers and that also makes the job more pleasant and fun to go to each day.

4. Adaptability

Employers seek employees who are adaptable and maintain flexibility in completing tasks in an ever changing workplace. Being open to change and improvements provides an opportunity to complete work assignments in a more efficient manner while offering additional benefits to the corporation, the customer, and even the employee. While oftentimes employees complain that changes in the workplace don't make sense or makes their work harder, oftentimes these complaints are due to a lack of flexibility.

Adaptability also means adapting to the personality and work habits of co-workers and supervisors. Each person possesses their own set or strengths and adapting personal behaviors to accommodate others is part of what it takes to work effectively as a team. By viewing change as an opportunity to complete work assignments in a more efficient manner, adapting to change can be a positive experience. New strategies, ideas, priorities, and work habits can foster a belief among workers that management and staff are both committed to making the workplace a better place to work.

5. Honesty and Integrity

Maintain a sense of honesty and integrity above all else. Good relationships are built on trust. When working for an employer they want to know that they can trust what you say and what you do. Successful businesses work to gain the trust of customers and maintain the attitude that "the customer is always right". It is the responsibility of each person to use their own individual sense of moral and ethical behavior when working with and serving others within the scope of their job.

6. Self – Motivated

Employers look for employees who require little supervision and direction to get the work done in a timely and professional manner. Supervisors who hire self-motivated employees do themselves an immense favor. For self-motivated employees require very little direction from their supervisors.

Once a self-motivated employee understands his/her responsibility on the job, they will do it without any prodding from others. Employers can do their part by offering a safe, supportive, work environment that offers employees an opportunity to learn and grow. Working in a supportive work environment and taking the initiative to be self-directive will provide employees with a better sense of accomplishment and increased self-esteem.

7. Motivated to Grow & Learn

In an ever-changing workplace, it is imperative to keep up with new developments and knowledge in the field. It has been noted that one of the top reasons employees leave their employers is the lack of opportunity for career development within the organization. Learning new skills, techniques, methods, and/or theories through professional development helps keep the organization at the top of its field and makes the employee's job more interesting and exciting. Keeping up with current changes in the field is vital for success and increased job security.

8. Strong Self – Confidence

Self-confidence has been recognized as the key ingredient between someone who is successful and someone who is not. A self – confident person is someone who inspires others. A self-confident person is not afraid to ask questions on topics where they feel they need more knowledge. They feel little need to have to impress others with what they know since they feel comfortable with themselves and don't feel they need to know everything.

The self-confident person does what he/she feels is right and is willing to take risks. Self- confident people can also admit their mistakes. They recognize their strengths as well as their weaknesses and are willing to work on the latter. Self-confident people have faith in themselves and their abilities which is manifested in their positive attitude and outlook on life.

9. Professionalism

Always exhibit professional behavior. Professional behavior includes learning every aspect of a job and doing it to the best of one's ability. Professionals look, speak, and dress accordingly to maintain an image of someone who takes pride in their behavior and appearance. Professionals' complete projects as soon as possible and avoid letting uncompleted projects pile up. Professionals complete high-quality work and are detail oriented. Professional behavior includes all of the behavior above in addition to providing a positive role model for others. Professionals are enthusiastic about their work and optimistic about the organization and its future. To become a professional, you must feel like a professional and following these tips is a great start to getting to where you want to go.

10. Loyalty

Everyone values others that they can trust and who exhibit loyalty. Loyalty in the workforce has taken on a new meaning. Gone are the days when employees plan on starting out and retiring with the same company. It is said that most people will hold between 8 – 12 jobs throughout their career. What does this mean in terms of loyalty in today's workforce?

Companies offering employee growth and opportunity will ultimately gain a sense of loyalty from their employees. Employees today want to feel a sense of satisfaction in their jobs and will do a good job when they feel that the employer is fair and wants to see them succeed. Although this may mean only staying for five or ten years in a position, employees can offer loyalty and make an important contribution during their time with the company.

More companies today encourage employee feedback and offer employees an opportunity to lead in their area of expertise. This gives employees a greater sense of satisfaction and a sense of control over their job. Empowerment encourages employees to do their best work since companies are displaying a trust and expectation that they believe in their employees to do a good job.

Offering jobs that encourage learning and the development of new skills also gives employees a sense of empowerment in the workplace. Aligning an employee's values with the goals of the organization will foster loyalty and a bond between employer and employee. Fostering good relationships within an organization and offering constructive ways to handle conflict provides a win – win situation for both employer and employee. Creating an organization that values loyalty within the organization can also work to its benefit by using the same techniques and strategies to establish loyalty with customers; and loyalty from customers ultimately makes for a successful business.

CHAPTER TWELVE

Failure Is an Option

Every idea from every discipline is an idea that comes from a natural, thoughtful, and endless expedition in which thinkers explore conventional knowledge, twist it ever so slightly in a new direction, or in some cases turning it upside down. That formula is not just the formula for original discovery, but also for sensible, everyday thinking for everyone.

As a society, we are so terrified of failure, that it paralyzes us from taking necessary risks to better our own lives, and the lives of everyone around us. Too many times we are taught to "not rock the boat", or to accept mediocrity as stability, and label it as success. While instead, we must teach the power of failure and how to fail effectively. We must teach that failure is a badge of honor, and something to be embraced, learned from, applied, and overcome.

Individuals need to embrace the realization that taking risks and failing are often the indispensable passages necessary to bring clarity, understanding, and innovation. By making a mistake, we are led to the fundamental question: "Why was that wrong?" By answering this question, we are deliberately placing ourselves in a position to develop a new insight to eventually succeed.

I look at an early example of failure, and the art of owning my failures in my own career. Early in my career, I was managing a construction project. And in my own arrogance of a project going all too well, I projected the profits at an unrealistic increase too early in the project. When the inevitable occurred, and we had issues that cost us money to resolve, impacting the profits, I was then asked by the CEO, Owner, and President of the company about this hit to our profits, when not a month ago we were forecasting an increase in profits...

The only answer I could give them was "I screwed up"... That's right... I made a mistake, but I can assure you that I learned from the mistake, and will not make it ever again.

That simple "owning" of it, rendered them completely powerless. I was right. I knew it, they knew it, and everyone else knew it. I made a mistake, I owned it, and I vowed to apply the lessons from it in the future. And that was the end of it.

I often refer back again and again to previous mistakes to celebrate just how significant they were to the growth of my abilities. If we foster an environment in which failing is a natural and necessary component in making progress, then we allow ourselves to release our own genius and share genuine ideas, even if those ideas aren't quite perfectly formed.

We put such an emphasis on success, that failure is not an option. And we hear this all the time. "Failure is not an option." But not only is failure an option, but it is a necessary component to growth. When was the last time you ever learned anything from doing it right? Conversely think about the last time you made a mistake, and what you learned from that experience.

So, what do we do? What has society taught us? Don't take risks, get a good job, keep your head down, and get through life. What the hell is that?! Where have all the entrepreneurs gone? They went to work for corporations. That's where. Why take the risk of failing, when you can command a fat salary as an employee, right?

Truly successful people have passion, and passion is what drives them. But what is it they are really passionate about? I will guarantee you that their passion isn't to avoid making any mistakes or avoid failure. Their passion is whatever makes them tic, regardless on the risk of failure. They know they may fail. They know the odds are likely overwhelming that they will fail… But they do it anyway.

I heard a quote one time that I thought was profound, yet profoundly simple at the same time:

"The work you do while you procrastinate, is probably the work you should do for the rest of your life."

When someone suggests to you to earn your living doing something you are passionate about, you immediately think of the physical actions of passion and not the mental ones. You mind says, what can I do that I am passionate about? But then your mind tries to talk you out of it by saying "there's no way you can make a living doing that."

You think that if you are passionate about cycling, that means you should open a cycle shop. If you are passionate about baking, maybe you should be a baker? If you love art, maybe you should be an artist?

Following that logic, would you then think that the CEO of Best Buy is passionate about selling electronics, or that a professional plumber is passionate about plumbing, or a furniture maker likes cutting and gluing wood?

It's a bit deeper than that. The passion lies not in the activity, but in the end result of the activity. It's the feeling you get from accomplishing an activity rather than the action of actually doing the activity itself. It's the feeling from overcoming the failures along the way, applying what we learned, and persevering. But our minds associate the activity, rather than the feeling we get from the activity.

You might enjoy running because you are passionate about competing and beating your race times. The sense of achievement it gives you pleasure, not the act of running itself, but the result.

A furniture maker produces fantastic furniture because he knows people are enjoying his produce and that motivates him to get up early each and every morning and work hard.

Your local plumber most likely isn't passionate about getting dirty and connecting pipes together, but rather delivering a smile to people's faces when he stops that leak or unclogs that drain. A passion for helping people.

What is the feeling of passion that you get after the activity itself, and how can you get even more of it? What is it that makes you feel a sense of purpose, or fulfillment? Don't look for the actual activity, the success or the failures, but look for the feeling after the activity, and pursue that feeling, rather than activities.

Your success and failures along the way are inconsequential when you finally realize your passion.

CHAPTER THIRTEEN

Strive to Be Working Class

If you were a child of my generation, then you grew up wanting to be the next Gordon Gekko, the next Wall Street giant, the next Master of Business who got filthy rich doing very little real work. Every facet of society in the 80s and 90s bombarded us with becoming rich, affording the finer things, driving the best cars, and flaunting your successes in the face of all the poor schleps working for a living. I guess this is maybe why movies like Wall Street, Goodfellas, and Casino were so popular. They embodied the philosophy of going out there and just taking what you want.

But what life has taught me more than anything is that it is all crap. Think about it... I have met people though the course of my life that were dirt poor, working class, and filthy rich... And without fail, every time, the people who are working class are the happiest. They are the ones living simply and accepting what life has thrown their way.

When you are poor, the stress of your situation can become overwhelming, putting you into a viscous cycle that, many times, is impossible to break out of without help. You are so consumed with day-to-day survival, that you cannot do anything to better your overall situation.

In the flip side, when you are rich, your life becomes diluted with the greed of holding on to what you have, accumulating more, and ensuring that everyone knows just how successful, rich, and great you really are.

The focus on accumulating stuff becomes more important than the relationships in your life.

People, who are working class… People who make up the masses of mediocrity… People who simply pay their bills, raise their families, and go to work every day… Now those are the people that are almost always happy. Those are the people who lend a hand to the poor and watch the spectacle of the wealthy as their lives unravel.

The term "youth is wasted on the young" is so true. What didn't I know? What didn't I appreciate? And what I could now tell my 22-year-old self… I often say that kids are stupid. Not to be degrading, or mean, but to be accurate.

The definition of stupid is:

> **To think that you know something, while being so clueless that you don't even realize what you don't know."**

And yes, kids are stupid, and yes, I was a stupid kid up until I was about forty. Because your forties are about when you begin to realize just how much you don't know.

What I wish I knew when I was 22:

- Stuff will never make you happy.
- You cannot put a price on doing something that makes you happy.
- Life is way shorter than you think.
- Tomorrow is never a guarantee.
- No one was ever remembered for how many hours they worked.
- Your legacy is what your actions project onto others.
- Forgive without the expectation of being forgiven.
- Love without reservations or conditions.
- You will become your parents… So, pay attention to them.
- Your values will define your reputation.
- Family is those who display love and loyalty before blood.
- You get one shot… Don't screw this up.

- Never choose your job over your family.
- Do what you must to support your family, but not at the expense of your family.
- If your spouse is not your best friend… Then you have the wrong spouse.
- Some people come into your life for a reason… Let them go when that reason is fulfilled.
- Some people come into your life for a season… Let them go when you grow apart.
- Some people come into your life for life… Treat them like gold.
- Experience and skill trumps education every time.
- Understand that you are no more special or unique than any other person in this world.
- Be the person that others will miss when you are gone.
- Be selfless.
- Make a life… Not a living.
- Say yes to your family often.
- Say no to work often.
- Choose to do work that helps others.
- Accept adversity, learn from it, and let it go.

Striving to be working class… Actually, setting a goal to be working class, on the surface, just seems so lame. It just reeks of commonplace, and settling for less than you could be… But it's so much more than that.

The truth is, that anyone can be rich. We all can be rich. But we already made the choice not to be. There isn't any one of us that can't make the choices required to become wealthy. Because in our hearts we know what we would have to give up becoming that person. If I had chosen to, I could have sought out jobs that paid large salaries and took me wherever I needed to go. But I know that I would have had to give up the things that I was not willing to give up.

Everyone wants to succeed in life. The real question is what is driving them? Is one driven to succeed because society tells them, or does their passion come from within?

Sometimes when trying to become so-called "successful", society can really hold you back. In the world we live in everyone wants instant results. Our society is driven by instant results...

But actual success, in any area of your life, is not instant. It takes years, sometimes decades. Some writers try to sugar coat stories of individual success like it happened overnight (people like Bill Gates, Steve Jobs, Mark Zuckerberg). What they don't understand is success usually happens when an individual finds something they are obsessively passionate about for a long period of time. The earlier they find this passion in life the more successful they usually are. The more like-minded people they surround themselves with, the better the momentum will be.

> *People say you must have a lot of passion for what you do, and it's totally true. The reason is because it's so hard that if you don't, any rational person would give up.*
> *- Steve Jobs*

The real question is, when you look at your life, your career, your path in this world, is it what you really want, or is it what you think society will approve of? In other words, if every profession in the world paid the same, and had the same benefits, would you still be doing what you are doing right now?

If a doctor, a plumber, a banker, as waiter, a speaker, as car salesman, all had the exact same income, and society status, which one would you be? Would you still take the same career path that you took to this point? I doubt it... So why are you doing anything other than what you are passionate about?

We tend to gravitate towards careers we are not passionate about, because they pay well, and have a higher social status. We seem to believe that this trade off somehow makes it all okay. It becomes okay to spend 40 years in a soul sucking job we dislike, because it pays well. We end up trading our happiness for things we can now afford to buy to fill that void, and we become masters at fooling ourselves into thinking that we are happy, when we clearly are not.

When we discuss the subject about society's pressure for success, we tend to focus on an individual's own success. What we do not realize is that people do not only feel the pressure to be successful themselves, but they also feel the pressure to have successful children as well. Success is no longer just a goal for oneself. Because one's children represent one's genes and/or one's parenting skill, success has also become a goal for one's children as well.

If a parent has a very successful career but their children fail to also have a successful career as well, they are deemed as a bad parent because they fail to guide their children down the same path to success. Even if a parent does not have a successful career, they are also deemed as a bad parent because they lack the capability to provide the means necessary in order for their children to succeed.

Society holds the parents responsible for the outcome of their children's success. If the parents do not have children who are genetically destined for success, the parents must provide an enhancing environment that would lead their children down the path towards success, such as enrolling them in a good school, helping them with homework, getting them a tutor, etc... When a parent fails to have successful children, they are considered a bad parent by our society.

So now, we have not only managed to suck the will to follow our own dreams and passions from our own lives, but we have managed to pass that on to our own children as well. Tell your children to follow their passions. Tell them to do what makes them happy and understand that all you need is enough income to live happy.

Living happy means doing what makes you happy. When you live happy, you really don't need much else. Your income needs are lower, and your expectations of society are lower.

CHAPTER FOURTEEN

The Social Economic Myth

So, there you are in the interview for your new job... The interview went well... You nailed it! A huge opportunity... You worked the last 20 years of your career, and all that college, ass kissing, working late, traveling over weekends, and family sacrifice is about to pay off... All those kid's birthdays you missed, all those anniversaries you missed, are all going to pay off.

So here it is... The offer. You are going to go from making $100,000 a year to $150,000 a year – with a performance bonus of up to another $30,000 a year. That's it! You made it! You're rich!... So, you've been taught.

Look. I'm not saying that a six-figure income isn't a respectable income, and that you shouldn't be grateful to earn it. Because it is great. What I'm saying is that for the most part, the people making $100,000 a year, work a lot harder, and sacrifice a lot more than the people making $40,000 and $400,000 a year. A job making right at that entry level six-figures is the most demanding place one can be.

These are the people that generally came from very little, or at least lower middle class, watching their parents struggle and kill themselves to make $50,000 a year. So, they decided to go to school and make something of themselves. They got the degree, sacrificed their family and lives to reach that six-figure mark, and be someone. Yeah, well I guess if being a slave to your work is someone?

Look. The social media would have you believe that there are two economic classes in this country... Rich and Poor. But the truth is that this is such total crap. And it is this crap that we all hear, and repeat, like a bunch of brainwashed zombies, that continues to perpetuate this myth. There are three economic classes in this country: The Survival Class, The Comfortable Class, and The Excess Class.

The Survival Class

The survival class are the people who are poor or borderline poor. These people are trying to raise a family on less than $50,000 a year, generally have no education, no skills, and no real direction. For whatever reason, they got a job, and just continued a path of entry level jobs. They either can't play the game, nor don't want to play it. They just simply found themselves in a cycle of survival, living paycheck to paycheck, and never were able to break that cycle.

The Comfortable Class

The comfortable class are the working class. These are the people who make $50,000 to $500,000 a year. These are generally the college graduates, or skilled tradesmen who entered a career path, and followed their path playing by all the rules, buying into all the lies, and moving forward. These are the people who have a little extra after each paycheck, and get comfortable, so they continue the path.

But don't kid yourself. The guy making $180,000 is financially no different that the guy making $80,000. The only difference is the size of the payments, the neighborhood, and the brand of car they drive. But at the end of the year, they have about the same size savings account.

The Excess Class

The excess class are the "wealthy". These are the people who make $500,000 plus annually, and truly have more than they need to live. These are the people who simply spend money on crap because they can, and to show others that they can. They certainly have more than they need to survive, and certainly have more than the middle class. Not to be confused though, these people span from mildly well-off executives, to the ultra-rich with millions and millions of dollars. But just the same, these people are wealthy, and have excess money beyond their need for a comfortable survival.

We all fall into one of these categories, and over the course of our lives, most of us may move up or down one level. But very few of us ever move across all three levels. Even though the carrot dangling out at the end of the stick would have you believe otherwise.

Yet there is one other part of the economic myth that no one tells you. This one is a little harder to see because they try much harder to hide it. Because without these two parts to the myth, the system crumbles, and we all become entrepreneurs… And God knows we wouldn't want that!

The bigger myth is that these billion-dollar mega corporations are taking advantage of their workers, working them into the ground, and spitting them out the other end. Oh, yes, it's true. Many of these huge corporations expect a lot out of their employees, and sometimes take advantage. But the truth is that unions, and the Government force them to give perks, breaks, time off, healthcare, gym memberships, and whatever else they can come up with. A company like Ford Motor, or Coke, or Union Pacific is so large they are lawsuit targets, and end up treating their employees quite well.

The problem companies are the regional corporations. Not the billion dollar a year companies, but the million dollar a year companies. The company where the founder may still be the CEO. These are the companies that expect employees to work as hard as the founder worked when he built the company. These are the companies that hire you for a $90,000 a year salary, dangle a $10,000 bonus in front of you, and then expect you to work 60 – 70-hour weeks, and sacrifice your family and anything that resembles a life for the company.

The truth is, if you wanted to work that way, you would have started your own company. But you were promised that six-figure income, insurance, and vacation time, and room to grow with the company. Who wouldn't want that?

The truth is, this whole "go to college, and get a good job thing" is setting our future generations up for epic failure. Not only are they taking on massive debt at an earlier age, but they are committing to working more for less, sacrificing time with their family, and doing a job, not because they are passionate about the work, but because it will ensure that six-figure income.

That, my friends, is why it is a social economic myth. We have all been sold a bill of goods. We have all, unknowingly traded our time, and family for the empty lie of getting more time and family, but instead getting more work, travel, and time away from our family. It's time we take a look at where we are and wake up.

There are 2,080 regular working hours in a year. That is 40 hours a week for 52 weeks. If you worked full time, all holidays, and took no time off, you would work 2,080 hours in one year. The average annual hours per person in the United States is 1,798 at an average wage per hour: $30.28.

We know that 20% of the employed workforce is part-time, working 20 hours on average. These are students, teens, second incomes, and such. These are primarily entry level jobs, generally filled by the survival class.

6% of the workforce is unemployed. These are the people who lost their jobs but want to work. Not the slugs who sit on their ass drawing a welfare check, playing video games, slinging drugs on the side, and generally just being a huge piece of crap.

This leaves 74% of the workforce to pick up the ball and run with it. These are the people who average 2,256 hours annually, and when you figure the standard holidays, and 10 days of vacation time, they are averaging almost 50 hours per week. That is average people. That means for everyone working their straight 40 hours, some poor fool puts in 60 hours. And I'll bet money he is on salary.

Here is how we stack up to a few other comparable countries:

United States

Average annual hours per person: 1,798
Average wage per hour: $30.28

United Kingdom

Average annual hours per person: 1,611
Average wage per hour: $31.27

Finland

Average annual hours per person: 1,578
Average wage per hour: $33.63

Luxembourg

Average annual hours per person: 1,565
Average wage per hour: $46.78

Denmark

Average annual hours per person: 1,496
Average wage per hour: $48.82

Ireland

Average annual hours per person: 1,469
Average wage per hour: $45.53

Belgium

Average annual hours per person: 1,446
Average wage per hour: $38.90

Austria

Average annual hours per person: 1,431
Average wage per hour: $36.63

France

Average annual hours per person: 1,392
Average wage per hour: $34.26

Netherlands

Average annual hours per person: 1,336
Average wage per hour: $42.67

Germany

Average annual hours per person: 1,330
Average wage per hour: $35.33

CHAPTER FIFTEEN

Re-programming Ourselves

" **C** haracter is destiny." Character shapes the destiny of an individual person. In his famous "I Have a Dream" speech," Martin Luther King, Jr. discussed a day when character was the measure of a person."

So what is this thing we call character? We all throw it around a lot, and say how much it matters, but what is it? Can we even properly define character? Think about it... It's easier said than done, which might be why it is so meaningful.

Rather than try to define character, and risk putting limitations upon its interpretations, I would offer instead, these objectively good human qualities, transcending time and culture to define character.

Wisdom

Wisdom is good judgment. It enables us to make reasoned decisions that are both good for us and good for others. Wisdom tells us when to act, how to act, and how to balance different virtues when they conflict. Wisdom enables us to discern correctly, to judge what is truly important in life, and to set priorities. Wisdom is acquired in small quantities over time. It cannot be taught, or acquired. Wisdom is earned, little by little, and eventually one becomes wise.

Fortitude

Fortitude enables us to do what is right in the face of difficulty. The right decision in life is often the hard one. A familiar adage says, "When the going gets tough, the tough get going." Fortitude is the inner toughness that enables us to overcome or withstand hardship, defeats, inconvenience, and pain. Courage, resilience, patience, perseverance, endurance, and a healthy self-confidence are all aspects of fortitude. We need to understand that we develop our character more through our sufferings than our successes, that obstacles can make us stronger if we don't give in to feeling sorry for ourselves, and just give up.

Temperance

Also known as self-control is the ability to govern ourselves. It enables us to control our temper, regulate our passions, and pursue pleasures in moderation. It's the power to resist temptation. It enables us to wait, and to delay satisfaction in in anticipation of the greater good.

A positive attitude

If you have a negative attitude in life, you're a burden to yourself and others. If you have a positive attitude, you're an asset to yourself and others. The character strengths of hope, enthusiasm, flexibility, and a sense of humor are all part of a positive attitude. All of us, young and old, need to be reminded that our attitude is something we choose. You can choose to be happy, or you can choose not to be… But it is, nevertheless, a choice.

Hard work

There is no substitute in life for work. Show me one single individual who achieved anything of substance without lots of hard work. Hard work includes initiative, diligence, goal setting, and resourcefulness.

Integrity

Integrity is adhering to moral principle, being faithful to moral conscience, keeping our word, and standing up for what we believe. Integrity is different from honesty, which tells the truth to others. Integrity is telling the truth to oneself. The most dangerous form of deception is self-deception. Self-deception enables us to do whatever we wish and find a reason to justify our actions.

Gratitude

Gratitude is not a feeling but an act of the will. We choose to be thankful, just as we choose to be positive. Gratitude is often described as the secret of a happy life. It moves us to count our everyday blessings. If you have all the fresh water you want to drink, shelter, and all the food you want to eat, you shouldn't complain about anything... Right?

Justice

Justice means respecting the rights of all persons. The Golden Rule, which directs us to treat other persons as we wish to be treated, is a principle of justice that can be found in cultures and religions around the world. Since we are persons ourselves, justice also includes self-respect, a proper regard for our own rights and dignity.

Humility

Humility can be considered the foundation of a whole life. Humility is necessary for the acquisition of other virtues because it makes us aware of our imperfections and leads us to try to become a better person. Humility is recognizing both our inadequacies and abilities and calling our abilities into service without attracting attention or expecting applause. Humility enables us to take responsibility for our faults and failings rather than blaming someone else, apologize for them, and seek to make amends. The key to character growth in life, is simply the humble willingness to change.

Every person's character is a gathering of strengths and weaknesses. Some of us may be strong in justice and integrity, but short on patience and forgiveness. For others compassion may come naturally, while courage is difficult. Persons of admirable character may differ considerably from one another. But for us all, our character is the result of some combination of strengths and weaknesses in these areas. If you have ever heard the term "Your word is your bond" that is the very definition of character being your currency. What is your currency worth?

Hold Each Other Accountable

It's easy to commit to be responsible for yourself, because you can control what you do. But that's the only person you can be responsible for. Right? After all, you can only control what you do, so how could you possibly be responsible for the next person? Everyone has their own free will, so everyone must police themselves. Right?

Wrong! The very fact that you have no control over anyone else is exactly why you must be responsible for them. If everyone answers only to themselves, then how do we avoid an absolute societal meltdown? The failure to hold each other accountable is the deterioration of any society, so we must stand up and hold each other accountable.

You may not have control over my actions... But you do have influence. And it is in that influence that you hold one actions accountable to that individual. You see, there is distinction between control, and influence. Control creates breakdowns, dissident, and chaos... But it is from influence that comes responsibility, self-control, and discipline. The more I try to impose my force on you, the more you will rebel. But the more influence that I may have, the more likely you are to come to the right decision on your own.

We must use our influence to hold others accountable before they act. We must influence others to be accountable to themselves, and to their community. We must as a society, not look the other way, and point out things that are inconsistent with good character, not let them spin it into something else. We must not be afraid to stand up and call a spade a spade. You'll be surprised how many others will step forward once someone else does.

Remember, if you are thinking it... Most likely someone else is too. So speak up.

Commit to Having a Great Day

Commit to having a great day every day, which requires that you embrace each day with no expectations.

Here is the cold hard truth of life... you are born, and then you die. All the rest is bullshit we make up to pass time. Almost everything you do each day only exists in your mind. 99% of your life as you know it does not actually exist.

Everything that does not naturally occur in nature is made up bullshit we thought up to keep from getting really bored while we wait to die. None of it is real, and none of it is essential to life. The only things essential to life are food, water, and oxygen. Those are very real, and I know this because you will not live long without any one of them.

Business doesn't actually exist. We made it up as an excuse to bargain for goods. Language is not real. We made it up as a way to communicate. Time doesn't exist. We made it up to measure how long it takes us to die. Your job isn't real. We made it up so you could formally trade service for goods.

Money isn't real. We made it up to value goods.

So, with this in mind, why is it that we enter into every situation with some expectation of what might happen? If none of it is really real, does the outcome really matter? Can we influence the outcome? Sure... But does it matter either way?

Of course, the outcome matters. But what we must do is keep in perspective the fact that 99% of what happens really doesn't matter.

Here is an example:

You went to the dealership to buy a new red sports car. You are excited and dreamt for weeks about this little red sports car. You get to the dealership and all they have is a blue sports car. Are you disappointed? Does it change anything about the experience?

Now imagine the same example:

You went to the dealership to buy a new sports car. You are excited and dreamt for weeks about this little sports car. You get to the dealership and all they have is a blue sports car. Are you disappointed? Does it change anything about the experience?

What was the difference? In both examples you got a new sports car that performed exactly the same and provided the exact same experience. The only difference was an expectation. Does it change anything about your life? It did if you went into the experience with an expectation of a red sports car. One of those scenarios resulted in a great day, and the other in needless disappointment.

Whatever happens… Happens, and it is okay, because you have no expectation. It is the unfulfilled expectations that will always lead to disappointment. When dealing with people, asking for something, and in day-to-day life, just open your eyes every morning, embrace the day, and enjoy what comes your way. Embrace every situation with the concept that both yes and no are equally acceptable.

How much stress and misery do we inflict upon ourselves trying to guide every outcome of every situation, get our way, and make sure everything comes out as we think it should? How much of that crap is completely out of our control? And how many times are we disappointed when it didn't come out the way we thought it should? Sometimes we need to step back, and let life come to us. We need to embrace situations for what they are and accept the outcome with no expectations. Not only will you not be disappointed, but you will be happier with the surprise of the way it all went.

I know, in some ways it sounds like a blissful ignorance, and in some ways it really is. But the alternative is to be this neurotic control freak who actually cannot control anything, and only succeeds in making life disappointing and miserable. I would much rather commit to having a great day each and every day, and then see what the day brings.

Let Go

Let go of your emotional connection to everything physical, and stop loving things... Instead pour that love and emotional energy into connecting with personal relationships.

This is a battle that goes all the way back to biblical times. For generations upon generations, man has had a fixation on the owning of things, and the importance of these things above all other things. It's just stuff, and the sooner you realize that the more stuff you have, the more miserable you will be, the sooner you can get on with life, and begin to build meaningful relationships with people.

In relationships, just as in every other aspect of life, the attitude in which you do things is at least as important as your actions. You are fully accountable for building relationships, so get out there and start doing it. Whether it is in your personal life, or your business, relationships are key to happiness. People do business with people, not businesses. And if you take a good hard look at your relationships in business, I would guess that your relationships in your personal life are a mirror image... good or bad.

Focus on friendship rather than a business transaction, or a personal relationship. Focus on building a friendship, in both business and personal relationships. Neither will be able to grow unless there is some level of friendship first anchoring the relationship. Then whatever the next logical step is, it will grow from that.

Make yourself happy instead of right. Start evaluating the things you do in a relationship based on whether those thoughts and actions are working. For example, you don't have to prove over and over that you know what you're talking about. Instead, choose a different sentiment such as tolerance, understanding or concern that does not escalate. By deciding to be happy rather than right, you will be receptive to other's attempts to de-escalate any potential hostility.

Letting Go of What You Refuse to Let Go of

We are all wired a certain way, and we all have something about us that makes us the way we are. While we all have many good qualities, we all have many not-so-good qualities. But there is always that one big one... That elephant in the room... We all see it, we all know it is there, but none of us make eye contact with it, hoping it will just go away, or no one else will notice it. Guess what?!? Everyone else saw it before you did!

Maybe you are always right, or maybe you make excuses to justify everything you do, or maybe you feel the need to protect your position all the time, or whatever... You need to identify it, and you need to be honest with yourself when you do identify it. I can't tell you what it is, but I can tell you it is not a good trait, and there is no way to spin it into a good trait. It is what it is... Identify it... Recognize it... And learn to let it go.

Be willing to recognize that which causes you to be the way you are and be willing to let go of it. You will always act in ways that protect you from your fears. If you can't figure out what it is that is causing you to be the way you are, look at your fears. Look at what event in your life made you really uncomfortable. Something that caused you to say, "That will never happen to me again... EVER." Identify it because that's it. Embrace it, understand it, and let it go.

The Corporate Ladder

The American culture dictates that the measure of professional success is making it to Executive VP, climbing that corporate ladder, and getting that one extra professional accolade to pad our resume.

We love to throw around job titles, and convince other coworkers and colleagues how successful we are, and how great our career is. We love to lie to each other, and fill our resume with all the most useless shit that can neither be confirmed, nor denied, but sounds great on paper.

Instead of putting the important things on our resumes, like, I saved the company $20,000 a year by eliminating waste, or I signed the largest client resulting in $100,000 of new revenue, we put things that don't mean crap on our resumes. Why? Because it's what we are supposed to do. It sounds good to the useless talking head reading it, and we tend to forget to think for ourselves.

So stand up and change it all. Reject the idea that ascension of the corporate ladder, job titles, and professional prestige are the measure of professional success. We are not saying to throw it all away. We are saying that it is more important to take stock in what we really do at work that makes a difference.

Leadership

There is so much good information about leadership. There are books about leadership with themes ranging from the military to Mickey Mouse; there are seminars, workshops, retreats, and entire conferences devoted to leadership, defining leadership styles, and even the best practices of other leaders. However, there seems to be a shortage of practical strategies for actually becoming a better leader. And there seems to be an even bigger shortage of leaders.

First, let's establish that leaders are not born. Leadership is a skill and can be learned like anything else. So if we aren't born with it, where do we learn it? We all learned the best technique for skill development and growth in kindergarten or preschool, during Show and Tell. The concept is simple. I have something; I am going to show it to you; and I'm going to tell you about it. These are the basics of how we learn from others. To really learn about leadership, we must watch what others have to show us.

Most leaders, supervisors, and managers are going way too fast. They walk fast, talk fast, and try to do too much at once. So it helps to physically slow down. Remember what we look like to those who we supervise. If we look like we're in a hurry, really worked up about something, and on a mission, then we probably are, and we do not seem at all approachable.

It also helps to mentally slow down and end the myth of multi-tasking. Multitasking continually comes up as a skill of great leaders, managers, and supervisors. I think this may be one of the biggest lies in business today. It is actually impossible to do "many tasks at once," which is what the phrase implies. I have tried, and I continue to try on a daily basis. To look around my office you can see the clues of my illness everywhere. I have three screens for my computer so that e-mail and spreadsheets are always on. I not only have to check an e-mail when it comes in, but I typically respond to it after only reading the first few words.

Leadership is a state of mind. It is not an activity to master. It is not a skill to hone. It is not a task to complete. Leadership is a state of mind that allows you to see with clarity, make decisions, and choose to be happy. A good leader isn't one who can rally the troops at the last minute to storm the castle. A good leader doesn't have to rally the troops, because the troops are already implementing the plan, and moving forward with or without you.

Leadership is a mindset that allows you to succeed without trying to implement anything to succeed. If you have ever seen those people who everything just seems to come together, the people who don't really try, the people who things just fall into place for... Those are the best leaders. They don't look like they are leading anything, yet they always seem to come out on top. Those are the kind of leaders we all must aspire to be. Great leadership has just become a part of who they are.

Reality Check

Okay... Time for a reality check. Some may call it a "Gut Check". Whatever you want to call it, if you have gotten this far in reading this, and not thrown it in the trash, then you are closer than even you thought you might be to actually changing some things in your life for the better...

Or at least you have an open mind, which still puts you ahead of most of the jokers out there.

So what's the reality check? And how do we do it? Simple… Just take a moment to step outside of your body for a moment. Are you someone you would be friends with? Are you someone who does what you love? Do you do what you love for the sheer love of it? Are you a person that puts others first? Are you a person who is generally happy all the time, and genuinely gets joy from life?

If you answered even one "maybe", then you might oughta wanna keep on reading. Because the cold hard truth is that if you didn't answer yes to those questions, then the fact is that not very many people like you, and you sure as hell don't like very many people. Being friends with you is work. And it is work because you make it work. You are not following your bliss, or genuinely enjoying what life has to offer. That makes you angry and hard to connect with.

You are going through life, working your job, making decent money, paying your bills, and being completely unfulfilled, because your soul is being depleted. You are working for the money, and not the joy of doing something you enjoy. Or you are doing something that you enjoy, and want to do, but in a way that is no fun. It is just as destructive to do what you want to do, but fight it and turn it into work.

Let's say for example you love to build furniture, it is something that is a bit of a hobby, and it feeds your soul. So you then decide to follow your bliss, open a big store, and plan to sell your furniture to the public. What you have just done is kill your dream, and turn something you enjoy into a job. Now you build furniture for the customers, and you are building furniture to pay the bills. You are over-extended, and just trying to turn out as many pieces as you can. You are no longer building the things you love, as you have to build what turns the best profit.

You didn't do a gut check along the way. If you had, something somewhere would have told you to stop and regroup. Something would not have felt right in your gut, and you would have known that you needed to take a different path.

Whether you are working a dead-end job, or trying to go it alone, you have to step back and do a reality check along the way… And often. You can never do too many gut checks. It is okay to question yourself and see if you are working within your own integrity. You know what your integrity is, and you know if you are within the boundaries that you should be. Step back and check yourself.

The Unimportance of Money

Have you figured out your obsession with one day having a lot of money? Really… We all dream of hitting the lottery, making it big, becoming rich. It solves all of our problems. Just look at the rich and famous, they are all happy, and content with their simple lives… Right?

When you really think about it and be honest with yourself: in the grand scheme of things, money is very unimportant and means little in itself. It's just little pieces of paper or numbers that show up on an ATM machine. It's not even real. It's just something we made up to assign a value to services. If all of society broke down tomorrow, all the money in the world would be useless. The new currency would be clean water and food.

However, as unimportant as it is by itself, it is the means by which the world functions. In our current world money is power, and it is the power that which we really crave. It provides comfort and in some cases joy, but more than anything else, it provides a freedom to do and acquire as we please. Money has the power to purchase, and influence, and that is where corruption truly lies.

Life is so complex and there are a million different things we need to worry about each day like our health, our families, or how we can help those less fortunate than us, that we really shouldn't have to worry about money. Life is hard enough as it is that money shouldn't make it any harder. My goal in life is to be happy, and to make the world a little bit better while I'm here. If there's any reason that I cannot reach these goals, it will not be because of money. If I'm unhappy in life because I can't find love, then fine. If I become sick or handicapped, then that is what was meant to be and I'm fine with that. If a train smashes me into pieces tomorrow and I die, then so be it, but I will never let money ruin my time on earth.

There are too many people in this world who work hard all their lives sacrifice, scrimp, and save all their money in retirement funds, savings accounts, stocks, and bonds only to die young and never get to use it. That won't be me. There are so many things to do and see in this world, and millions of people who could use a few dollars here and there. When I die, I will be as I came into this world, totally broke, but utterly happy and satisfied that I have lived my life to the fullest... I will have spent my time trying my best to make my family and friends happy, all made possible by the fact that I did what made me happy, regardless of the money.

Dream Small

What the hell? Dream small... But all of the hundreds of inspirational Facebook posts everyday tell me to dream big, grab the world by the balls, and go out in a blaze of gunfire to the cheer from the crowds. Why would I ever want to dream small? That's exactly why you want to dream small.

We are put on this earth for a very short time. In that time here on earth would our time be best spent impressing others, and grandstanding for those whom we not only don't know, but we think are huge douche bags anyway? Why do we spend so much of our time giving a shit about what people we don't like, think about us? And so little time molding what our kids think of us?

If you are anyone who has ever spent any time at all in the limelight, had any notoriety at all, not necessarily even fame, just become very well-known... You know that once the very brief fun wears off, and it does quickly... You know that you really just want to crawl off and hide from everyone. You long for the days of obscurity and being just a regular "Joe".

You see, it is in the small things that we derive the greatest joys in life. The small things like a baby's laugh, a new puppy, your mom's pot roast, a sunset, fresh baked pie, the smile of a loved one, a nap, the simple things that we cherish most.

It is not in the grand that we find happiness, because it is always these grand events that take on their own little set of mini dramas. Everyone wants a piece of your moment, so they are always working to tear down and destroy what it is that you worked for. So, you learn to take joy in the simplest of places and events. You will get a lifetime of joy out of watching sunsets with someone you love every day... But you will get no lasting joy from closing a big deal or building a huge corporation to be envied by many.

Be the Eternal Optimist

What would you say if I asked you to describe the preverbal half glass of water? To most of us, the answer is either "half-empty" or "half-full." Historically, your answer would label you either an optimist or pessimist.... until now.

Is it half-empty? Or half-full? Unfortunately, the question is fatally flawed. Supposed to test a person's perspective on life, the glass-half-whatever scenario does more to test the assumptions of the questioner than the optimism of the subject. Most of us shout out the answer, failing to reflect the most important aspect of the situation: the objective of the glass owner.

If you were to re-evaluate the situation of the glass with the objective of the owner of the glass in mind, you would realize that your answer depends entirely on what they are trying to accomplish. If the owner's goal is to "fill the cup" of water, then "half-full" is indeed the optimistic response. Conversely, if the goal is to "empty the cup" then "half-empty" is truly seeing things on the brighter side. Both of these answers, as they pertain to the situation, are correct and full of opportunity, and therefore both answers are indeed the optimistic point of view.

So as you can see, this illustrates the difference between an optimist, and the eternal optimist. The optimist sees the glass as half full and completely recognizes that others will see the glass as half empty and accepts that.

However, the eternal optimist refuses to accept that there could be a negative or pessimistic option. They instead seek out to understand the objective prior to rushing to judgment or shouting out the answer that many would expect a "leader" to give.

The eternal optimist will break this question down and examine the entire situation. The more we understand about the various, often conflicting, objectives in play: the more prepared we are to identify opportunities and forge clear-cut, measurable paths to success.

Focus on the Positive

In a world of negativity, drama, scandal, unemployment, and bad news, it can be a real challenge to remain positive. It can be very easy to forget that no matter how bad, and negative things might be, there is always a glimmer of good… A reason for hope… A positive spin that you can put on this.

A grateful mindset wields a powerful influence on your outlook. Not only does it make you feel good in the moment, it also shifts your focus in a positive direction. Turn your attention toward the good things in your life, and as you focus more on what you are grateful for, you will worry less about anything that may be lacking. As a result, you will experience a more universal sense of happiness!

Being happy is not about situations or outside energy. Happiness is a decision we make from within ourselves. Why not make up your mind to embrace happiness, starting now? Let your personal identity become the very concept of happiness.

Subconsciously, the word problem says, "Life is not as it should be." This causes us to interpret that our energy should be channeled toward mending something that's gone wrong. On the other hand, the word challenge actually inspires us to get up and meet this encounter. Instead of trying to restore a breakdown, we search for a new opportunity. Seeing an experience as a challenge will focus our attention on a positive outcome.

A journey is an adventure of discovery, and shouldn't that be the definition of your life? When we are on a journey we look forward to new and unfamiliar experiences. On a journey we are full of optimism because we are filled with the anticipation of a magnificent adventure. This is the perfect attitude to live your life.

When you continuously feel rushed and scattered, it can be difficult to remain optimistic. Focus on simple pleasures to restore a sense of balance to your life. Pause to really taste your food or enjoy a beautiful sunset, to remind yourself of the joy of simplicity. After all… the entire concept of this book is rooted in simplicity.

Find a few minutes each morning to clear your mind and then think encouraging thoughts about the day. Take some time to look forward to everything that you might enjoy and let your optimism flow into your entire day.

Be with positive people. Use the power of peer encouragement to feed your sense of optimism. The attitude of the people around is a powerful force, so seek out the company of those with a bright personality and let yourself be influenced by their optimism.

Stop watching, reading, or listening to the news. If you can free yourself from this negative influence, it will change your life. Without that general daily dose of depression, you will find it easier to focus on positive things in life.

Negativity

The word No has got to be the single most destructive word on the planet. We all use it every day, over and over, not giving it a second thought. But have you ever really thought about what the word No does to the human spirit? There isn't any grey area, there isn't any room for negotiation, and there isn't any room for compromise. It is just an absolute shut down of whatever it is directed at.

No, I don't have the money to launch a new business. No, I don't have time to write a book. No, I'm not smart enough to learn a new language. No, you can't go out and play. No, we don't have time to paint the house. No, No, No... No compromise, no options, no place to go.

Why are we always saying No? Is whatever it is, really that much of an absolute? Is there really no other option? No other compromise? Or are we just too lazy to go the extra mile? Or are we just conditioned to say No?

Oftentimes, we tell ourselves No because we think someone might not approve of our actions, and God forbid, someone does not like us, or our decisions. It is very important to remind ourselves that we live our own lives, mistakes, and all. Just because someone else tells us not to do something, doesn't mean we shouldn't.

I'll be the first to admit that I used to complain about everything; my job, my dog, my home, my friends, my car, whatever. Complaining, only allows us to make more excuses, and we are no longer in charge of our destiny, our situation takes charge.

A lot of negativity originates from the idea that we can't do something we've never tried before. The more you challenge yourself to do new things, the less you will tell yourself 'No, I can't do that.'

Everyone, no matter who you are, has dreams and goals, but most people think they don't have the time to pursue them. Even if you are raising ten kids and have two jobs, you can always find time to devote to your passion. Devoting time to your goals will boost your self-esteem and give you the courage to say 'yes' to more goals.

Challenge Yourself

This is a topic that is, in my opinion the most misunderstood. Challenging yourself seems to always be associated with some kind of quest for greatness, bordering somewhere between immortality, and the impossible. The fact is, that challenging yourself is neither the mark of greatness, not anything less than possible. Challenges can take the form of the most mundane things. They can be anything from challenging yourself not to swear around the kids, to challenging yourself to not max the credit card on your next vacation.

For a challenge to mean something, we must first conceive of something in your heart, that you really want to do. Then make that your duty... Devote yourself to its achievement, paying no attention to distractions, or what others may think. This is the path to self-control and concentration of thought. This is a skill that you will refine over time, thereby allowing you to take on challenges that are of much greater importance.

For even if you fail, as you may, the strength of character you develop is the true benchmark of success. Strength is developed by stretching yourself, asking more, through effort and practice.

Just as you can build muscles in the gym through resistance exercise, a person can make oneself strong by exercising in correct thinking. You see, it is not the challenges that you really want to master, it is the art of taking on challenges, seeing them through, and coming out a better person on the other end that you seek.

Standing at a Crossroads

So, if you've gotten this far, you might be finding yourself approaching that crossroad. That point in your life, not where you must choose a new path. But where you begin to question what you have known to this point to be fact. You may find yourself questioning the very foundation that you built your career and life upon. You may in fact be wondering if you have made all the right decisions, and if there is even any room for reconsideration of any of them.

Consider this... What if I told you that there is no past, and no future, but there is only today? And what if I further told you that there isn't even a today, but only a present? And what if I told you that the present was only a millisecond of time? Would it make any difference to you?

No one ever lives in the past, or for the future. We can only live in the present, and we can only do it a millisecond at a time. You see, that is all we have, because right now is the present, and every millisecond that passes is a new present time. That's all you get…

The past is not a measure of time. It is merely a memory or record of something that happened in the present some time in history. At the same time the future is not a measure of time either. The future is merely an anticipated present time yet to come. While we affix a name to the past and future to make it easier to track our place in the universe, the only time that can exist is the present. And the present is a millisecond of time, so why not pay a little closer attention to that? Because it will literally be gone in the blink of an eye.

So now we find ourselves back at that crossroads, evaluating what we know to be true, what we thought we knew to be true, and realizing how little we actually know to be true. Here we stand, contemplating our decisions, weighing our options, evaluating everything that has gotten us to this point… Now What?

Choosing Your Path

So, tell me… To this point, have you chosen your path in life, or has life chosen the path for you? Many times, it is our inactions that shape our lives far more than our actions. For most of us, we end up in dead end jobs, we hate, marriages we hate, careers that have nothing to do with our education, incarcerated, working as a traveling carnival worker, or whatever, not because we actually made the choice to do it, but because life made the choice for us, and it was just easier to go with it.

We all come to crossroads in our lives. Many more times than we know, because we are usually so caught up in the drama, and crap that becomes a day in the life of us, that we don't even see it. There is opportunity all around us. Every day we are confronted with opportunities to change our lives, to improve our situations, to take a new path… But we don't see it.

Sometimes it's blinding fear, sometimes we are comfortable with our chaos, so we ignore it or don't recognize it. But it's there, none the less.

Oh sure, you can remember every time that you came to a crossroads, and actually took action. Yet we never seem to know how we got to where we are the times we didn't choose to be on the current path, yet here we are, right in the middle of that path… Ever think about that?

No more! From this point forward, we must not only take an active part in shaping the direction of our lives, but we must make active decisions as to where we want to go, and how we want to get there. We must decide what is important to us, and what is the legacy we want to leave behind for our children? Do we want to be remembered as that hard-working son of a bitch that provided all of the material things, but was never there physically or emotionally? Or do we want to be remembered as that fun-loving, life affirming, yet responsible person who lived every millisecond of life like it was the only one they had?

Choose your path wisely. Evaluate every aspect of where you came from, where you are, and where you think you are going. Evaluate what you missed out on as a child, and what your children might be missing out on right now. Evaluate the big picture and think about what changes might need to occur in order to implement changes at this level. Evaluate what is most important to you, and work backwards from there…

And when you are done… Understand this could take months to do… And when you are done, ensure that everyone close to you understands, agrees, and is willing to walk that path with you… Then choose your path.

I Don't Care What Others Think

It's just so easy to get caught up in the rat race of impressing others with your stuff. Oh I know… I had the 4,500 square foot house, the Hummer, the BMW, the 34-foot cabin cruiser, the 55 plus foot houseboat, the Rolex, bla bla bla… Impressed aren't you?

Yeah, me neither. Actually I'm a little embarrassed, because along with all that really cool stuff came a ridiculous house payment, a couple ridiculous car payments, boat payments, boat slip rent, bills, insurance, oh and let's not forget $600 a weekend in boat fuel, and on and on and on...

You see, the fact is that no one gives a crap what you have. They only care about their own stuff. Now of course I loved the boats, and toys. They did make me happy. But I would have been just as happy with a 20-foot boat instead of a 55 foot boat.

Now, I'm not saying don't get the stuff that makes you happy... Actually quite the opposite. Get the stuff that makes you happy, do what makes you happy, and have fun with it. Just make sure that it is something that is comfortably within your reach. Own your stuff... Don't let your stuff own you. If you can't pay for it, don't buy it. If you need a loan, then you probably need other priorities first.

Make sure that when you buy stuff... The stuff you just can't live without... Make sure that you are buying it for the right reasons. Don't spend five times more to buy a Mercedes, when a Ford will do just fine. Don't buy a $10,000 Rolex, when a $50 Timex will do just fine. Don't spend your weekends popping bottles in the VIP section, when a 6 pack at the lake will do just fine.

We are not saying don't splurge on yourself once in a while, or not to treat yourself well when you earn it. What we are saying is to keep it simple. Do what you do for you, not for others. Own what you can own because you can afford it, and because it makes you happy. No other reasons! Do what makes you happy, and fill your life with experiences, memories, and excursions. No one can ever repossess your life experiences, so focus your time and money on that.

When you dress to impress, drive expensive cars, live in big houses, and throw money around like you have it, all you do is make yourself look childish. You become a target for moochers and losers who feed your ego, and leave you broke. No one gives a crap about you once they can no longer get something from you.

I have driven everything from BMWs to Hummers, to Dodge trucks to Jeeps, to street rods... And the best vehicle that I have ever had was a 12-year-old Toyota with 150,000 miles on it. Why? Simple... It ran like it was new, and it was paid for. Dependable and debt free... Yup, the best damn car I ever had!!! What do you think about that?... Never mind, I really don't care what you think about that. It makes me happy, so screw you, find your own thing that makes you happy.

Simplicity

In the West we have a tendency to be profit-oriented, where everything is measured according to the results, and we get caught up in being more and more active to generate results. In the East, especially in places like India, people are more content to just be, to just sit around under a tree for half a day chatting to each other about absolutely nothing.

It is the simple this that create lasting happiness. Living a simple life will give you freedom from stuff and over-consumption, which always seems to be where our problems stem from. Concerns for our stuff, worry about protecting our stuff. Spending money to maintain our stuff. It just never seems to end.

Living intentionally and with integrity keeps you grounded and mentally in tune with your moral fiber and promotes the creation of more life experiences. Focusing on a simpler life promotes caring for the Earth and Earth's inhabitants, gives you spiritual discipline to live ethically.

Changing Your Perspective

Your perspective is the way you see yourself, your spouse, your pet, your world, and the world as a whole. Your perspective is your reality. Perspective can be a wonderful thing, and a horribly destructive this, all at the same time.

Perspective is reality... This is very powerful, because one person's perspective on a situation isn't really reality, because they could be wrong.

Right? But then again isn't that person's perspective actually their reality, whether they are right or wrong? You see perspective can be a very powerful thing that can shape everything.

For example, let's say you have this wonderful cute little dog that snuggles you, licks your face, and is the perfect companion to you. This dog is awesome, always waiting at the door to greet and love you every time you return home and sleeping at the foot of your bed protecting you, always on watch for out of the ordinary noises. This dog is perfect!

Now my perspective, as your neighbor, of this little bastard dog is that it is an annoying little turd, who barks non-stop while you are gone, pisses on my bushes, and growls at me every time I see it outside. My perspective of this dog is that it is a real jackass.

Who is correct? We both are in the context of our perspective of the dog. So my point is, that perspective is reality. If you like something or hate something it is generally a result of some experience or something we were taught. In most cases these perspectives are burned into our minds from our parents because we grew up watching them in situations, and learned our responses to situations from them.

Change your perspective and change your life. Your perspective on a situation or your life generally forms your outlook, attitude, demeanor, and response to what comes your way. Whether you embrace something or reject something is determined by your perspective on it. Don't like where your life is? Change your perspective. Don't like where your career is? Change your perspective.

Believe in Yourself

Ever wonder what holds you back? Ever wonder why you do what is simple? Ever wonder why you do what you are comfortable doing? The answer is simple... You don't believe in yourself.

You see, most of us go through life, some extremely successful, doing what we are comfortable doing. What we know. What comes easy to us. Unfortunately, that which does not truly challenge us becomes very unfulfilling. Look at your own life… I know that I am a very talented and experienced construction manager with experience working on several world class construction projects. Projects that any one of you have seen, heard of, and visited. But as good as I am at it, and as easy as it comes to me, it is so unfulfilling to me. I could make tons of money doing it, but I just didn't enjoy it.

So why did I spend over 20 years doing it? Simple answer because I didn't believe I could do anything else. I didn't believe in myself. I only believed in my education and experiences and didn't trust in me.

So how do we begin to believe in ourselves? Set goals. When you set goals, you have control over what you are trying to achieve. It keeps you focused, grounded, and gives you a way to measure progress. Recognize when you achieve your goals, so that you will build your confidence. Consider reasons when you fail. Everyone fails to achieve some goals, but if you learn from the failure, you will be more likely to succeed in the future.

Use realistic expectations to judge your success. Do not expect to run a four-minute mile, until you have trained and conditioned to run a four minute mile. You can judge your success by looking at the gap between where you are and where you want to be. This perspective helps you measure what remains to achieved. You can also evaluate by looking at the progress you've made from past times. This helps you know how far you have come. Both perspectives are valid.

Listen to everyone's feedback, but never let them persuade you that you should give it up, or that you are less than you are. Some critics will tear you down to make themselves look superior to you, while others will offer acute guidance to help you make changes to improve yourself.

Give your time and energy to others. When you do this, you will receive encouraging responses and respect from everyone. This helps you to build a foundation for self-confidence, which is crucial to believing in yourself. Don't give up on your dreams, goals, or aspirations for you never know how right they truly are until you put them into action. Believing in yourself is the key to success in life.

Follow Your Passion – Do What You Love

Do what you love, and the money will come… Well, not so fast. Unfortunately, while we would all like to believe this, but it's not really always true. Sometimes what we love just isn't profitable, in which case we have to find an alternative, or something related to what we love, to actually make a living at. But none the less, follow your passion, and make every responsible attempt possible to make a living doing what you love.

If you find that your passion is kite flying, and you can't seem to make a living flying kites, then maybe you need to look at something related to the kite industry. Maybe kite design, kite making, running a hobby shop, or an online kite enthusiast group… But my point is, that just because you can't make a living flying kites, it doesn't mean you have to become a sewer drain cleaner or some other job that you will hate. Be creative and continue to follow your passion where it might lead you.

The real point to this is actually to choose a profession that is rooted in your passions, rather than the money. You see, I spent many of my younger years struggling to make a living, and struggling to make any real money, just getting by, and saving. Then, like a light switch came on, all of a sudden making money really was not that hard. You see, once you learn how to make money, it is easy. It is much different than learning your job skills and applying them in trade for payment. No it is the actual skill of making money. Once you learn how to do it, life becomes a lot more fun, and a lot less work.

I can't really explain to you how to make money, because it is the application of a different concept for us all. But I can tell you that it starts with the release of the notion that you must make money. As long as you set out every day to make money, you will struggle to make money. However, as soon as you release that fixation on the money, and focus on that which you enjoy, and that which is fulfilling to you, and others, that you suddenly find yourself not concerned about money.

Is it that you are no longer driven by the money? Is it that the money is no longer the center of your focus? Is it that you found something other than money to be passionate about? Is it that your attention has been harnessed for the good of you? Is it that you found something that feeds your soul instead of your bank account?... Yes...

Now take that passion and run with it. Let go of money, and what money can buy, and focus on your happiness and passion. It is as simple as this. Make a list of everything that makes you happy but money cannot buy. Be honest with the list, and don't cheat by putting two or three things on the list. Fill a page, be silly, be whimsical, be honest. If you can't honestly come up with fifty things in life that make you happy, but are absolutely free, then you are not trying. Just start writing with no regard for who might read the list, with no regard for something being stupid. If it makes you happy, right it down. Stupid shit makes me happy... Before you know it you will have pages of things written down.

Now make it a passion to acquire, do, or fulfill everything on that list. Don't stop until there is a checkmark next to everything on the list. Once you complete the list, you will have some sense of what it means to follow your passion. You will know that you can achieve happiness regardless of money and stuff.

Be Enthusiastic

Enthusiasm enables you to do things in an enthusiastic way which helps you achieve your goals, and acts as the fuel to get you on your way through your day. Being enthusiastic will keep you interested, and happy, as well as compel others to get involved with whatever it is that you are doing.

The best definition of courage is going from failure to disaster without losing your passion. So based on that, we could imply that passion also helps build courage, and it is in that courage that you can actually reject the pressures of society, stand up, and walk away from that which is wrong with society, and the pressures of societal consumerism that keep us in debt, burdened, and unhappy.

So why are some people more enthusiastic than others? What is the secret behind their enthusiasm? The foremost thing enthusiastic people possess is an attitude of eternal optimism. If you are enthusiastic, every problem is a challenge which you will face with absolute courage and self-confidence. Obstacles become your steppingstones to success.

Enthusiasm gives you an unbelievable energy to live with focus, sincerity, and passion. When you are passionate it feels good for you to go about your day with never ending energy and strength. Enthusiasm is the end product of positive thoughts, and it never allows negative thoughts to enter your mind. Positive thinking and behavior make you feel enthusiastic in whatever you do.

When you get wake in the morning with enthusiasm you find that you look forward to the day with enthusiastic anticipation and you exude a contagious energy. If on the other hand you do not like your job, life, friends, or your coworkers, you become dull and the effort you put into your life and work shows is just second-rate as there is no enthusiasm in it. You immediately become someone who is not fun to be around, and people will actually avoid you.

Do not let your mind slide into negative thoughts as you will find it difficult to do anything with optimum energy. You should like what you are doing to be enthusiastic, but you also must realize that if you are enthusiastic, you will like what you are doing.

It is not enough if you are enthusiastic in your work, you need to be enthusiastic in your family life as well to enjoy total happiness. If you do not enjoy good relationship with your family, there will no friendly interaction between family members, and everything becomes routine.

When you are enthusiastic, you are fun to be around, and there is laughter, jokes, and good times. When you are enthusiastic, positive, active, and full of life your brain is active, and when your brain is active it never lets you descend into negative thinking.

Live With Purpose

Living with a purpose can be the most satisfying part of living, and it can be the most miserable part of living. So, what is the difference? The purpose, dummy!

Why are you here? Who cares? The fact is that you are here, and you have no idea how long you are here. So, make the best of it. Many people get hung up on the question of why are any of us here? What is life all about? What is the grand master plan? How do I find the purpose of life? You want the incredibly simple, obvious answer that so few people ever seem to come up with? Really? You haven't figured it out yet on your own? Really?

Simple… What is the purpose of my life? Whatever I choose. Yup! That simple. The purpose of your life, your existence on this earth, your mark on the world, your legacy, and your use is whatever you choose it to be.

We are self-aware creatures with the ability to make independent choices and put into action anything that we want. So where do we get this notion that we are supposed to look to the stars, or some other intrinsic power to tell us what our purpose in life is? Why it that the obvious answers are never the ones we come up with? Your lot in life is whatever you choose it to be, so figure out what makes you happy, and do it. Pay no regard to what society tells you is acceptable, what your family wants you to be, what your friends think of your choices… Just do it. (Obvious disclaimer suggests that it is legal, responsible, and moral).

If you family disapproves of your purpose, tell them to accept it or stay out of it. It's not your choice to alienate them. It's theirs. You are simply being who you are, doing what makes you happy, and living your life as you see appropriate to your moral compass. If they can't accept it, that is their problem, not yours.

If your friends don't like the direction of your life, and the choices that make you happy... Then it sounds like you need new friends. Most likely your friends are not really some deep connecting with you as a person, but more of a social connection to where you are in your life at any point in time. Friends come and go. Look at your life and look at how many came and went, and why. Most likely they were a product of convenience tied to a social status or social connection. Don't believe me? Change your social status and see how many friends remain.

Oh sure, there are a couple people that become lifelong friends. Generally about 2% of the people that you are ever friends with become lifelong friends. Cherish these people. They are special, and they likely get you better than you get you. I have always said that I have about 4 friends, and hundreds of acquaintances. Those few friends are people that are constants. You most likely even interact with them less than you do with your social friends. But these are the people that you can call at 3 a.m. to help you bury a body... Not that I've done that... Really.

So ignore everyone and everything, be selfish, and choose your purpose based your needs, wants and desires. Put it into action, and let the cards fall where they may. As long as you have been honest with choosing your purpose, you will be happy no matter what comes your way.

Work Hard – Relax Even Harder

When stress at work begins to pile up, it can be difficult to imagine a time when you will be able to relax. Busy days and appointments may seem like the only way for you to make sure that all of your deadlines are met, but they aren't good for your long term health or happiness. If you want to be able to give your best to your work, you need to be able to recognize the signs of stress and look for ways of easing it.

Happy, healthy workers are the ones most able to continue meeting the demands of their lives. Does this mean pushing yourself to work sixty hour weeks is necessary? Maybe? Sometimes it may be necessary. But refusing to take time off can actually damage your work, rather than improve it.

Ensure you're able to give your best, by making sure you take ample time for yourself. Work hard when you need to, but balance that work with the right amount of relaxation and play.

Exercise is another good way to work stresses away, so why not see if you can add an early morning swim or post-work gym session to your routine. Not only does exercise leave you feeling more invigorated in the short term, but it also helps you fall asleep. Something many people who are stressed and working too hard have trouble with.

It's also essential that you do your best to use the PTO time provided to you. Don't work bank holidays or vacation, and make sure you book yourself a few week-long breaks a year. A short time away from work can give you a new perspective. If you work for yourself, remember to schedule time off. Most self-employed business owners just wait for down-time, but that down-time never comes. Make a point to schedule time in large blocks. A few long weekends here and there is not enough. I assure you that everything will not fall apart in your absence. Really! You're not that important.

Make sure you travel during your breaks and resist the temptation to take your smartphone or laptop with you. Instead, think of your holiday as a chance to recharge your batteries and let stress drain away. From adventure breaks to relaxing holidays, you'll find that some time away is sure to help you work all the more efficiently when you return. Do not check your email, text, or phone messages. Leave someone in charge of making decisions on your behalf, trust them, and deal with it when you get back. Odds are, even though they may make different decisions, they will still be good decisions.

There is a book called "The 4-Hour Workweek" by Timothy Ferriss. This is a great read for those of you who have not mastered your schedules. If you are booked all day, every day, and there just don't seem to be enough hours in the day to get it all done, then you need to read this book. The truth is that you are not nearly that important. You are not nearly as good at your work as you have convinced yourself that you are. You are really not good at it at all. You are simply shitty at managing your schedule. You let everyone else manage your schedule and your time for you. You let everyone else dictate where your time will be spent. Instead, why don't you try forcing everyone else to do their damn job, and stop wasting your time, so you can go to the beach?

Know Yourself

I have taken many business and leadership courses over the years in an effort to become a better leader, manager, and business professional. And many times, I've been humbled to discover things about myself that I didn't want to know. I learned that I believed that I needed other people to like me in order to be happy, and that I was a pleasant, warm person, when in fact I wasn't. As surprising as learning these things was, perhaps even more surprising was that learning them surprised me. How is it that I didn't already know these things? Why do the things we discover about ourselves generally surprise us? How is it our view of ourselves so often turns out to be entirely wrong?

Could it be that we are both right? We are how we perceive ourselves, yet we are also how others perceive us, at the same time. When we look at ourselves and use the term "we" toward ourselves, consider the "us" that lives beneath our conscious. Not only are we composed of multiple "selves" often in conflict with one another, but we are generally not aware of the other "us".

Okay... Kinda deep? It isn't really. Think about it like this. You are you, and you are always you, right? So, is the "you" that your mother sees, knows, and loves the same "you" that your boss sees, knows, and pays to do work? No, of course not. But you are still you, right? We are all made up of multiple personas that act in ways appropriate to the situation we find ourselves in, yet there is still only one of us.

The conscious mind is a great interpreter. It's drawn into making sense of the world and everything in it. Constantly assessing situations and determining how to react to those situations. Unfortunately, it prefers diluted explanations that keep its view of the world within the parameters that you set for your life. That's why we all have a hard time thinking outside the box. We know what we know, and we are comfortable in that world. The unknown is the scariest thing on earth.

Given our conscious mind's tendency to make shit up to validate what we believe to be the way it is, generally at the expense of the truth, it's no wonder we're generally wrong about why we actually do the things we do, and the type of people we actually are. Add on top of that, our ego-driven need to appear to be all things honorable and decent, and we find ourselves mixing a potent recipe for significant self-delusion.

Slow Down and Enjoy

Isn't it ironic that our modern lives with all of the technology continually invented to improve our lives, make things easier, and more efficient, doesn't actually save us any time? In fact, the more time saving technology we invent, the less time we have. You see, we fail to use this technology to free up more time. Instead, we use that new time to do more and more things, and so our lives are more fast-paced and frantic than ever.

Life moves at such a fast pace that it seems to pass us by before we can really enjoy it. However, it doesn't have to be this way. We have the right to rebel against a hectic lifestyle and slow down to enjoy life.

A slower-paced life means making time to enjoy your mornings, instead of rushing off to work. Pour a cup of coffee and watch the sunrise. An average sunrise only lasts 26 minutes, depending on where you are in the world. You can spare 26 minutes to sit, relax, gather yourself, and start your day.

Take time to enjoy whatever you're doing, to appreciate the outdoors, to actually focus on whoever you're talking to or spending time with, instead of always being connected to a phone or laptop, instead of always thinking about work tasks and emails. It means single tasking rather than switching between multitudes of tasks and focusing on none of them. You've heard the term "Jack of all trades, and master of none"? Well, that is the American professional workforce. We all think we should be multi-tasking, when in fact we should be focused on what we are doing.

Slowing down is a huge conscious choice, and not always an easy one, but it leads to a greater appreciation for life and a greater level of happiness. Slowing down, often requires a lifestyle change, and making choices to eliminate certain things from our lives.

Do less. It's hard to slow down when you are trying to do a million things. Instead, thinking about it as choosing to do less. Think about it as choosing to focus on what's really important, what really needs to be done, and let go of the rest. Put space between tasks and appointments, so you can move through your days at a more leisurely pace.

Be present. It's not enough to just slow down, but you need to actually be mindful of whatever you're doing at the moment. That means, when you find yourself thinking about something you need to do, or something that's already happened, or something that might happen, bring yourself back to the present moment. Focus on what's going on right now. Focus on your actions, on your environment, on others around you, and how you are being affected in the moment. Take a moment to look around and take a mental note of your surroundings, the room, the chair, the sounds, smells, and textures. Look at the artwork, landscape, or whatever might be around you. Be in the moment.

Disconnect sometimes. Don't always be so intense. If you carry around a phone or other mobile device, shut it off. Better yet, learn to leave it behind when possible. If you work on a computer most of the day, have times when you disconnect so you can focus on other things. Being connected all the time means we're subject to interruptions, we're constantly stressed about information coming in, and we are at the mercy of the demands of others. It's hard to slow down when you're always checking new messages coming in. Schedule a specific time to check message and stick to it.

Focus on important people. Too often we spend time with friends and family, or meet with colleagues, and we're not really there with them. We talk to them but are distracted by devices or thoughts. We are physically there, but our minds are on things we need to do. We listen, but do not hear, because we're really thinking about ourselves and waiting to talk. None of us are exempt from this, but with conscious effort you can shut off the outside world and just be present with the person you're with. This means that just a little time spent with your family and friends can go a long way, and a much more effective use of your time. It means we really connect with people rather than just meeting with them. At the same time, do not waste time with people that are not important to your life. These are the time sucking leaches that steal your life, your time, and your thoughts.

Appreciate nature. Many of us are stuck inside homes, offices and cars most of the time, and rarely do we get the chance to go outside. And often even when people are outside, they're talking on their cell phones, and not enjoying the outdoors. Take the time to go outside and observe nature, take a deep breath of fresh air, and enjoy the tranquility of water and grass. Exercise outdoors when you can, or find other outdoor activities to enjoy such as nature walks, hiking, swimming, etc.

Eat slower. Instead of cramming food down our throats as quickly as possible, leading to overeating and a lack of enjoyment of our food, learn to eat slowly. Be mindful of each bite. Appreciate the flavors and textures. Eating slowly has the double benefit of making you fuller on less food and making the food taste better. Enjoy the experience.

Drive slower. Appreciate your surroundings. Make driving a peaceful time to contemplate your life, and the things you're passing. Use your commute to plan your day in the morning and recap your day at the end. Don't use the time to read emails, return messages, and continue to work. Driving will be far more enjoyable, and much safer, and you'll use less fuel too.

Single-task. The opposite of multi-tasking. Focus on one thing at a time. When you feel the urge to switch to other tasks, pause, breathe, and pull yourself back.

Breathe. When you find yourself speeding up and stressing out, pause, and take a deep breath. Take a couple more. Really feel the air coming into your body and feel the stress going out. By fully focusing on each breath, you bring yourself back to the present, and slow yourself down. It's also nice to take a deep breath or two.

Success

Just to think about success. What is success? This is the Big Question. Success comes from the Latin "successus", which means an outcome. For each of us the answer is different as we all have different outcomes in mind.

When talking about success in general, we must forget what we have already learned. We must remain open to the concept of success, but not necessarily as we define success today. Success is a feeling of pure satisfaction deep inside oneself, a feeling brought on by an achievement that is both honest and challenging. Successful is when you have accomplished thousands of these successes and are motivated to go for thousands more. It is an internal feeling, not an external accumulation of things. It can't be measured by any outward appearance, and only you can know if you are a success.

When we talk about success in general, there are two interpretations: success in your eyes and success in the eyes of other people. I can own a business, a big house, a private jet or whatever and be a success in the eyes of other people, but in reality Success to me could mean being happily married to the same woman for many years and the rest just happens because I believe that behind every good man is a good woman.

One could give loads of examples, but at the end of the day success is deep inside oneself. There is always going to be somebody to think or say, "You should have done things differently" or "You could have done better." Forget about these people if you feel in your heart, you have given your best; if you feel satisfied with your achievement, this is success.

Warning! One of the prices of success is the more outwardly successful you become, the less comfortable your unsuccessful friends will be with you. Success is here for everyone; it doesn't matter who you are or where you come from. It is not your background, the way you were raised, your education or any environmental situations that make you a success. It is what you do with what you have that makes you a success. You may have heard the expression "The Black Sheep of the Family." This guy has the same background, but he doesn't have the same values or work towards the same goals as the rest of the family.

Success is often wrongly associated with material wealth. This is purely superficial. What good is it if a man gains the world and loses his soul? As I said, it is what you do with what you have that makes you a success. Ask yourself "Why not me?"

Where Your Thoughts Go, You Go

We all know that insanity is continual repetition of the same cycles expecting new results. Doing the same things every day with the same people and thinking the same thoughts is going to leave you with the same results. Therefore so many of us get into a rut.

We all have that internal voice that is continuously going on in our heads; this is the voice that sends our beliefs to us the whole time. The voice that says "It's too cold to get out of the bed today" or whatever it is your voice says to you. Hopefully your voice says things like "Early to rise makes a man healthy wealthy and wise." Do you see the difference two totally different thoughts can have on one of the first actions of the day?

You are your own most important critic. Your opinion of yourself is the most important opinion you can have as you move forward. The most important conversations you will have as you move forward are with yourself. You have to be in control of this self-dialogue; you must get it to work for you not against you.

The mind is what separates people who succeed and are happy from those who don't. When you decide to change your inner world, your life can go from ordinary to extraordinary. We have control over our minds; we have the power to decide what to think at any given moment. The mind is divided into two separate parts. The Conscious and the Subconscious. This internal dialogue comes from the subconscious, and it is your subconscious that you must continually keep in check.

Your mind has a default setting. For some the default is good, and for others it is destructive. You must recognize your default and keep it in check. Changing your self-limiting beliefs is like changing the default setting on your computer. You just go and do it. All personal breakthroughs begin with a change in beliefs, so changing to self-empowering beliefs is a must in order to move forward.

The three best ways of doing this are

1. Visualization
2. Affirmation
3. Association

Visualization:

This is as easy as day dreaming; it is imagining, even fantasizing what you want. It is also useful to visualize your past successes to reinforce these and help you build self-confidence. Our minds play an important part in the creation of our experience and that it is possible to program our mind to act in a certain way to gain positive results.

Affirmation:

This is as easy as talking to yourself instead of listening to yourself. Affirmations are short powerful statements in the present tense. These statements put you in conscious control of your thoughts. When you say, think or hear these affirmations, they become the thoughts that create your reality. Affirmations become your conscious thoughts. Just talk to yourself in a positive manner, and you can convince yourself of almost anything. It's kind of like Bart Simpson says, "It's not a lie, if you believe it."

Association:

You get your brain to associate bad to your self-limiting belief. You must feel deep down that this belief has brought you bad in the past, is causing you bad now, and will continue to do so if you don't change it right now.

Next you associate great pleasure with the idea of adopting a new self-empowering belief.

Strength

It's hard to believe, but most people don't know their strengths and talents. Many of us guided by our parents, teachers and later work environment become experts on our weaknesses. We spend our lives trying to repair these instead of developing our strengths. A strength is a continuous excellent performance in an activity. This activity we do well consistently, and we really enjoy doing it.

Everyone seeks strength. Just as some lift weights for physical strength, your internal strength also builds from enduring hard work, setbacks, and continuously working at it. Just as a bodybuilder builds their physical strength, you can build your inner strength through persistence and exercise. Exercise your mind, your self-control, your emotions, and your internal strength to become stronger.

CHAPTER SIXTEEN

Living in a Disposable World

It appears that today's civilization has evolved to such an elevated level of awareness and prominence, that we do not have time to fix things. It is cheaper and easier just to toss it in the trash and buy another one. It's probably outdated anyway... Right?

We think that we've become a better society than in the past (because we all know history will never repeat itself) by becoming more aware about the "Global Warming" propaganda, bragging about how we're now "eco-friendly", and how activism and "caring" magically makes us better people, giving us the right to do whatever we want, as long as we "care". It seems that we've become more consumers than conservationists, hypocrites instead of honorable, and just plain wasteful rather than prudent.

This ties directly back to our lack of pride in producing quality, and lack of craftsmen, creating, not just products, but taking pride in creating something that they are proud of. We look back at generations who lived through the great depression of the 30s, and we now call them hoarders. This is a generation that fixed everything. They saved coffee cans, jars, butter containers, and anything else that could possibly be repurposed. Anyone who remembers going to their grandparent's house and seeing their grandmother washing out a plastic cottage cheese container so she could store leftovers in it, knows what I am talking about... Hell, today's generations won't even eat leftovers, let alone save a cottage cheese container!

Try to repurchase the same model of a cell phone you've grown accustomed to a year after getting it. It's impossible unless you lost your phone within six months of buying it. Own a phone for over a year and the world has already moved on, no matter how much you liked the simplicity, ergonomics, or features of the one you had. You must turn to something smarter and operating with more Gs than the old model. We, the customer in the phone store, are shepherded through the technological ritual of the various "new" models whether you want it or not. Like livestock, driven toward the purchasing corral by a pimple-faced, annoying, douchebag, younger than my kids who keeps telling me how "awesome" this phone is for streaming, face-timing, and downloading… Completely missing the point that all I want is a fucking phone! Not a pocket laptop computer.

It is the same for everything, televisions, DVD players, cars, even vacuum cleaners. A good version of most every appliance is turned over to obsolescence at a frightening rate. Most things get replaced well before they need replacing, simply because something new and better is out there. Most things break before they should. Nothing gets fixed anymore. Nothing lasts. Do you realize that people used to make a living in appliance repair? It was a real living breathing business operated by a craftsman. Gone! Why? Because it's just easier, and cheaper to just throw it away. In the 80s, Madonna wrote an anthem about the materialism of American culture. Now, in addition, we have a culture of disposability.

I worry about the direction society is leading our children. Really, think about it. On one hand, all we as a society do is talk about recycling, like it is some new thing, yet everything is designed to be tossed in the trash.

The thirty something's are complaining about it because we, and older generations, grew up with the expectation that a piece of electronic equipment costing a few hundred dollars or more would be with us for a good number of years. Younger people have grown up expecting that they need to upgrade frequently to keep up. They do not think it is foolish to buy something new when they have a similar something older, because it does a few more things or works a little faster. On the contrary, a child's technology has become a measure of social acceptance the way tennis shoes, and clothing brands were among the "popular kids" twenty years ago.

Companies have made electronics a fad industry with massive marketing campaigns to kids and pressure in our culture to have the latest thing. The disposability of these products is an intentional strategy by companies to keep you coming back, like a heroin addict needing your next "fix" of the latest technology. Maybe buyers should consider how much they need them.

Microsoft is not spoiling our children any more than McDonald's is making them fat. We remain, for the time being, the wealthiest nation in the world. Technology companies have made their products just affordable enough for most income levels, and just appealing enough for a credit card charge to those that can't quite afford them. American parents are generous and want to give their children the best of everything. While an admirable sentiment, it is precisely the reason that these generations are so lost, and misguided.

I have seen this many times, and many of you may have seen it as well. It can be found all over the internet. But each time I see it, I find myself reading it, and feeling a bit embarrassed, and kind of awkward... I'm not sure who first wrote it... It wasn't me, but it is worth reading as a testament to our society, and just how stupid we really are.

> Checking out at the supermarket recently, the young cashier suggested I should bring my own bags because plastic bags weren't good for the environment. I apologized and explained, "We didn't have this green thing back in my earlier days."
>
> The clerk responded, "That's our problem today. Your generation did not care enough to save our environment for future generations."
>
> She was right about one thing—our generation didn't have the green thing in "Our" day. So, what did we have back

then? After some reflection and soul-searching on "Our" day, here's what I remembered we did have....

Back then, we returned milk bottles, pop bottles and beer bottles to the store. The store sent them back to the plant to be washed and sterilized and refilled, so it could use the same bottles repeatedly. So, they really were recycled. But we didn't have the green thing back in our day.

We walked up stairs because we didn't have an escalator in every store and office building. We walked to the grocery store and didn't climb into a 300-horsepower machine every time we had to go two blocks. But she was right. We didn't have the green thing in our day.

Back then, we washed the baby's diapers because we didn't have the throw-away kind. We dried clothes on a line, not in an energy gobbling machine burning up 240 volts — wind and solar power really did dry our clothes back in our early days. Kids got hand-me-down clothes from their brothers or sisters, not always brand-new clothing. But that young lady is right. We didn't have the green thing back in our day.

Back then, we had one TV, or radio, in the house — not a TV in every room. And the TV had a small screen the size of a handkerchief (remember them?), not a screen the size of Wales. In the kitchen, we blended & stirred by hand because we didn't have electric machines to do everything for us. When we packaged a fragile item to send in the mail, we used wadded up old newspapers to cushion it, not Styrofoam or plastic bubble wrap.

Back then, we didn't fire up an engine and burn fuel just to cut the lawn. We used a push mower that ran on human power. We exercised by working so we didn't need to go to a health club to run on treadmills that operate on electricity. But she's right. We didn't have the green thing back then.

We drank from a water fountain or a hose when we were thirsty instead of using a cup or a plastic bottle every time we had a drink of water. We refilled writing pens with ink instead of buying a new pen, and we replaced the razor blades in a razor instead of throwing away the whole razor just because the blade got dull. But we didn't have the green thing back then.

Back then, people took the bus, and kids rode their bikes to school or walked instead of turning their moms into a 24-hour taxi service. We had one electrical outlet in a room, not an entire bank of sockets to power a dozen appliances. And we didn't need a computerized gadget to receive a signal beamed from satellites 2,000 miles out in space in order to find the nearest pizza joint.

But isn't it sad the current generation laments how wasteful we old folks were just because we didn't have the green thing back then?

Trends in our society already seem to indicate that younger workers have less loyalty to their jobs. They are less likely to get married. They are also likely to carry more substantial debt and save little for their retirement, a continuing legacy from their predecessors. It is frightening to think that careers and relationships, even families somehow become more easily disposable in their adult lives, simply a product of the disposable world we live in.

CHAPTER SEVENTEEN

Putting America Back to Work

How do we put America back to work? Every politician in the country has an answer for this one, right? The answers range from cutting taxes, raising taxes, cutting interest, changing policies, job programs, increase trade, cut trade, on and on and on... bla bla bla bla... I got news for you. All the politicians are wrong. I don't care what they are saying, I don't even need to hear it. They are wrong. You see, if they knew anything at all about business and job creation, they wouldn't be politicians, and they would have actual jobs that produce something of value for this country.

The answer to this is so simple, it pains me that so few understand it. If America is going to once again, become a world power, we need to understand this one simple concept: We need to get back to creating things. As anyone that lived through the great depression of the 1930s knew. There is no job beneath you.

In the 1930s, any job was a great job. Today, we seem to have this entitlement that there are some jobs that are beneath us, and for the purposes of doing this work that no one else will do, we can look the other way on illegal immigration. I mean really, without the immigrants, who would do it? And we wonder why every other country in the world hates us. Mmmmm... Go figure.

This means we need to teach our kids that being working class is the noblest profession, and learning a craft is something that no one can ever take away from you. If you have a skill, are willing to work, and have an ounce of work ethic, you will always have a job and be able to feed your family. What a great feeling it is to lay your head down at night with rough hands and a sore back, knowing that you actually did something that day. You have pride in your work, and you are proud to show everyone what you have accomplished.

In less than 200 years, America grew from a handful of colonies to become the greatest nation in history. In a few hundred years, we surpassed nations that are centuries older than America.

So how did we do that? The two main components that made that possible were the conviction of our people and the very freedoms that we based our belief structure on. The people in American have had a can do, nothing is impossible, spirit. Starting with the American Revolution, we have always conquered adversity, often in the face of overwhelming odds.

We have more rights and freedoms than anywhere else in the world. Our freedoms are considered inalienable rights, not privileges granted by government, but rights. Our freedoms are the envy of the world. Every item in the bill of rights is precious and designed to ensure the immortality of our liberty.

Our founders came from societies where government controlled its citizens, not the other way around. They had a solid understanding of the consequences of unchecked power. Our constitution was crafted specifically to limit the scope of government to prevent its infringing on individual liberties.

Our constitution is a brilliant document, filled with foresight and understanding, that has withstood the test of time. The principles embedded in the constitution are the foundation of our greatness. In America, each citizen can control his or her destiny without fear of interference by government or others. Our government was formed to serve the people rather than vice versa. Our government was designed to play a minimal role in people's lives.

Our doors have always been open to people from anywhere in the world who want to come here legally to work hard, contribute, and assimilate into our society. America's reputation as a melting pot is derived from the fact that people from every walk of life can work together to create an unstoppable force for good.

Only recently, has this "melting pot" concept been twisted into some kind of tolerance mandate, where we must not only accept, but tolerate the degradation of the foundation of this country in an effort so as to not offend others. This political mandate of tolerance is the root of the decline of this country. It is the notion that there are no absolutes, and that we must understand, and tolerate any behavior, in an effort to accept other cultures. I reject that notion in its entirety, as American culture is unique to America, and we are not required to tolerate cultures that are at odds with American culture.

In America anything is possible. America is great because it offers its people unlimited opportunity to succeed by bringing their dreams to reality. In America, success requires hard work, determination, and persistence, not permission. We are constitutionally protected to prevent the government from confiscating the results of our labor, and we must ensure that the concept of redistribution remains a form of confiscation, for which our very constitution protects us from.

America has been an engine for unprecedented productivity, growth, success, and progress. Our economic system has been responsible for more civilization transforming innovations and discoveries than any other country. No other country has even come close, and many other systems have failed miserably. This is not the time to relinquish that honor to China, the Middle East, or some other obsolete, irrelevant country. This is the turning point we need to regain that pride and honor, to once again rise as the world's greatest superpower.

America has a big heart. Sometimes too big, but nevertheless, whether in this country or elsewhere, we help those who cannot help themselves. Americans are first on the scene in the wake of natural or civic disasters. We are there with food, supplies, medical aid, and money. Our brave soldiers travel the globe defending those who can't defend themselves.

In America there are no problems that we can't solve. Any obstacles we may face do not blemish our greatness. It is our greatness and legacy of prominence that enables us to overcome adversity and become even stronger in the process. Every day, be thankful that you have the opportunity to benefit from the legacy of this country, and that you have the opportunity to change the direction of the woes that this society finds itself in. Don't take for granted that which people in other countries can only dream about, because they envy you and what you have, and their hatred of you is the manifestation of their envy. So be proud and give them something to envy once again by living your life without limits.

So how can we get back America back to WORK? I think it starts at home with you. Teach your kids to work, do not give them things, and make them earn them. They will appreciate them more and take better care of them. Be willing to say NO, you do not need that and do not borrow money to buy things. Grow a garden and teach your kids this is a good thing. Live off the land occasionally, go fishing and eat what you catch, so you can be more self-sufficient. Bake a loaf of bread rather than buy one. I'm not advocating moving to the mountains and living in a cave. But do these things once in a while.

Take your kids on a camping trip, and don't take all your food. Instead take fishing or hunting gear and teach them that if we don't catch our dinner, there won't be any dinner. Hunger is the single best motivator I have ever witnessed. Research has proven that in catastrophic event, it only takes 4 days without food or water for your delightful friendly neighbors to become a deadly threat to you. I'll say it again, hunger is a great motivator.

Encourage your kids to work over the summer and even during the year. Teach your kids to volunteer, and do for others occasionally, without any pay. Teach them to fill their karma account, because difficult time will find them, and they need all the help they can get. I heard someone once say, that good deeds only count if no one knows who did them. The next you go through a drive through, buy the meal for the car behind you, tell them you only ask that they pass the favor onto someone else.

Start your kids thinking about a skill related career, a craft rather than a trade, a passion rather than a job. Not only are these careers rewarding for the soul, but they pay well, have great benefits, and teach entrepreneurial skills to go out and start your own business. Teach self-reliance rather than depending on the village to raise your kids. Teach them to take pride in what you do, and who they are. If it is worth doing, it is worth doing right… And if it's worth doing, it's worth doing right now. Don't put things off until tomorrow… It may never come.

Our country will not be great again, until the silent majority begins to embrace their work, take pride in working for a living, and start coloring this countries collar blue again. Let's end the whiney entitlement excuses, and attitudes, and stop looking for someone else to hand us everything. It all starts with you and what you can control.

CHAPTER EIGHTEEN

Ten Core Values of Living a Meaningful Life

1. A person's character is their currency. Spend wisely.
2. Be responsible for yourself, and the next person. The failure to hold each other accountable is the deterioration of any society, so stand up and hold each other accountable.
3. Commit to having a great day every day, which requires that you embrace each day with no expectations. Whatever happens... Happens, and it is okay, because you have no expectation, recognizing that it is unfulfilled expectations that lead to disappointment.
4. Let go of your emotional connection to everything... Not everyone. Personal relationships are what matters in both business and personal success.
5. Be willing to recognize that which causes you to be the way you are, and be willing to let go of it. You act in ways that protect you from your fears. Embrace that which you fear, understand it, and let it go.
6. Be a student of life, every day of life, continually learn from everyone and everything that you encounter. You will hold formal and informal education as having equal value.
7. Reject the assessment of material prosperity as a valuation of personal wealth.

8. Reject the idea that ascension of the corporate ladder, job titles, and professional prestige are the measure of professional success.

9. Leadership is the antidote to being a follower. Leadership is a state of mind that allows you to see with clarity, make decisions, and choose to be happy. You don't have to have a following to be a leader, you just have to take on the role of leadership and lead the way.

10. Feed your soul. When you operate from a genuine place, you share your soul with others. This requires that you feed your soul with that which makes you whole.

CHAPTER NINETEEN

The Silent Movement

For the last five decades, high school graduates turned away from careers in the trades, leaving U.S. corporations who rely on talented skilled tradesmen and women to make up their workforce scrambling to figure out what to do.

Well, it turns out that there is hope. There is a silent movement of today's high school students rediscovering the trades. It's quiet, it's not widely reported, and it's not liked by the academic elite... But it is happening none the less.

High school students and 20-somthings are finally starting to question the narrow path laid out by educators, gaining an interest in careers in the trades. They are realizing that the path of higher education leads to crushing debt, underemployment, and a nonessential workforce. Additionally, this generation is starting to think about life in a much simpler light. They no longer strive to be ultra-wealthy, buy exotic cars, and have huge homes, which all come with high loan payments. They want a simpler life, living modest, reducing their carbon footprint, and enjoying a more moderate lifestyle. They are focusing less on stuff and more on experiences, and quality of life.

Entire generations of skilled workers are simply missing from the trades. Skilled, talented, trained professionals in their 30s and 40s are nearly impossible to find. That means when the current generation of tradesmen,

men, and women in their 50s retire, all the responsibility to get the jobs done right will fall onto the shoulders of men and women just now entering the workforce, just learning their craft, and these kids are starting to see that.

Demographic momentum, cultural changes, a global pandemic, an unprecedented shift in how people live and work, housing shortages, a rise in household wealth, and widespread new technology adoption, as well as a persistent shortage of skilled labor, are all combining to create the most dynamic, exciting, and opportunity-filled moments in the modern history of the trades.

The trades represent careers with high job satisfaction driven by a connection to the meaning of the work, high pay, and high levels of entrepreneurship. This movement is fueled by hard work, a good attitude, a rejuvenated focus on work ethic, grit, determination, and the joy of completing a job well done. Trade organizations are recognizing the connection between what their trades offer and what workers are seeking during the Great Resignation, as we see a narrative change around trade labor and start to reverse the labor shortages that have impacted the trades for years.

This is the most exciting time for the skilled trades in modern history both because of the pandemic and because of the "Great Resignation." The Great Resignation could provide great opportunities for skilled tradespeople in America. Study after study, survey after survey is tapping into the growing discontent amongst American workers. People want to feel more connected to their jobs and to their work.

That connection between the work and the meaning and value of work has always been strong with skilled trades and is now more relevant than ever before. This is the opportunity to redefine the trades as craft and begin to eat away at the challenges of perception around this essential, vibrant, and important work.

The trades have a wonderful array of benefits to offer, there is a pronounced shortage of skilled labor, and opportunity abounds for the innovative entrepreneurs that can grow and scale businesses in this unique time.

While recruitment needs to be more adaptive to the shortages and tap into the current labor movement, the trades are innovating. The pandemic resulted in severe supply and labor constraints across virtually every sector; however, tradespeople have rapidly adapted to the situation with new tools, technology, payment options and planning methods.

As the economy continues to grow, people will choose to spend that new wealth on new homes, cars, and improving their lives. All this pent-up and planned spending needs a supply of available skilled tradespeople to do the work, and the opportunities are limitless for those willing to tackle the industry's challenges in the years to come.

CHAPTER TWENTY

Working Class TV Show

G rowing up on a small farm in the Midwest, I went to a trade school for heating and air conditioning, working in the trades, and worked my way up in the large-scale commercial construction management business. I am currently the Director of Construction for one of the largest, most respected contractors in the country.

Spending over 30 years in this business, I have grown passionate over the struggle of finding qualified trades people who want to work in the industry. As a result, I work very hard to promote the trades, and vocational training on as many platforms as I can.

I was approached by the JUL-TV network to help consult on, and produce another show called "The Money Machine" which is similar in concept. Through the process, the network suggested that maybe I should be doing my own show, so we went down that development road, and came out the other end with a show concept... And "Working Class" was born.

Working Class is a show, targeting the 18-35 age demographic that explores different trades, and non-traditional career paths that our schools refuse to teach. We spend a day with a trade's person, working with them, learning the trade, and their story. Our hope is to expose a viewer to another career path that excites them and instills some passion.

As leaders, we all need to keep talking about it with vocational schools, unions, high schools, and community leaders. As with any issue, it all starts with awareness and understanding. But deeper than that, we need to be doing something as parents and communities. We need to demand our schools bring back vocational training. We need to stop brainwashing our kids that they need to go to college. College isn't for everyone. We have convinced an entire generation that the only path to success is through a college degree in a field that has no jobs, low pay, and lifelong crushing debt. It is absolute insanity.

We must stop convincing every one of the stereotypes and preconceived notion that the trades are low pay, hard work, and 2nd class. We need to talk about the pride that comes from craftmanship and building something beautiful. The pride that comes from being a part of creating something.

I believe the younger generations; the women and minorities are all looking for something different. They are not as focused on money and status as generations prior. They are more focused on experiences and adding meaning to their life. They want to make a difference, and this is a career path that provides purpose and makes an immediate difference in lives.

How many retail workers, baristas, fast food employees, unemployed and under employed college graduates do we have to churn out before we follow the data? A career in the trades with pay for your education, take half as long, provide a retirement path, and have a higher starting pay. Stop following the masses and encourage your kids to forge their own path.

Providing Value...

Everyone tells you to work longer, work harder, get certifications, become more educated, etc. And that is all good if it helps you provide more value. But if your value is hard work and long hours, or a degree or certificate, I would ask, what is the value? Does that inherently make the company more profitable?

I would challenge you to think bigger. Think more holistically. Understand what people need and provide that.

The lesson I want people to learn, is to plan for tomorrow but live for today.

- Do what you want to do today.
- Plan to die broke, you can't take it with you
- Take your vacation
- Buy that boat
- Eat that cake
- Be a person of value to others
- Fill your karma tank
- Be responsible… But live your life

www.ingramcontent.com/pod-product-compliance
Lightning Source LLC
Chambersburg PA
CBHW021421210526
45463CB00001B/484